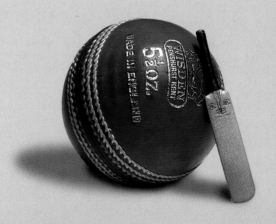

# THE QUEEN'S DOLLS' HOUSE

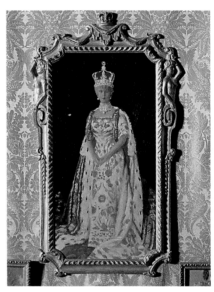

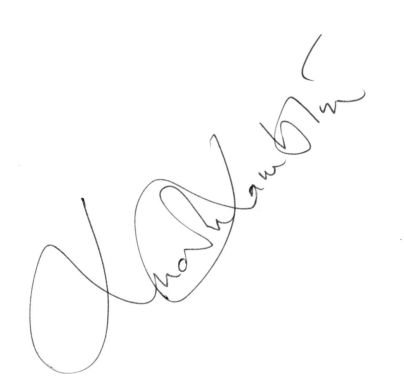

Lucinda Lambton

# THE QUEEN

## CONTENTS

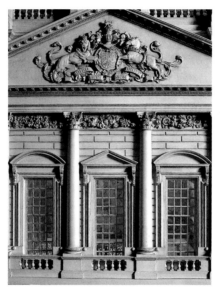

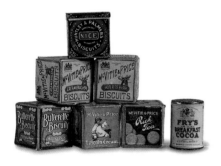

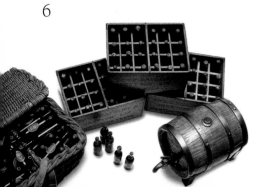

# 'S DOLLS' HOUSE

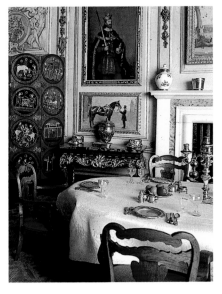

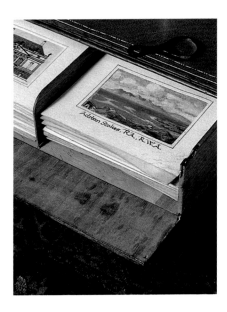

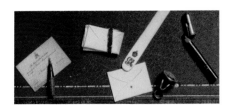

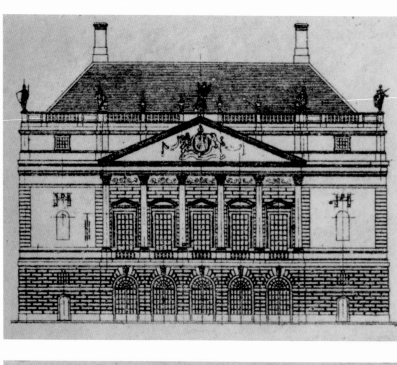

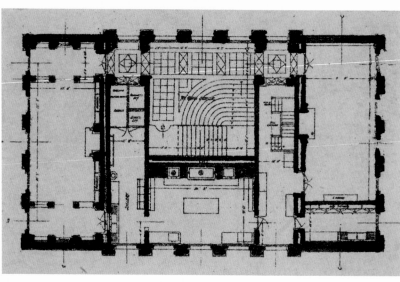

*The atmosphere of the summer of 1914 in England ... pervades*
*a few of Lutyens's later country houses ... its essence, distilled but*
*pungent like an old potpourri, is perhaps most distinctly sensed in ...*
*Queen Mary's Dolls' House ... The end was no doubt coming, but till it*
*came let us live, they said, as fully, as well, as handsomely as we can,*
*and build so that we leave at least a memorial of the civilisation*
*we inherited and perfected. In the Dolls' House Lutyens epitomised*
*that view ... the way of life of another great age was passing away.*
*Let it be portrayed exactly, at a scale of one inch to one foot,*
*for the delight of children and historians forever.*

Christopher Hussey
*Life of Sir Edwin Lutyens*, 1950


*This is where we raise a shout and burnish our escutcheons,*
*The better to reflect the glory of Sir Edwin Lutyens.*
*Mighty things he can erect, from a Dolls' House to a Dam, Sir.*
*He's George's Royal Architect and Mary's little Lamb, Sir.*

Anon
Written to celebrate Lutyens' degree of Doctor of Civil Law at Oxford, 1934
To be sung to the tune of 'Good King Wenceslas'

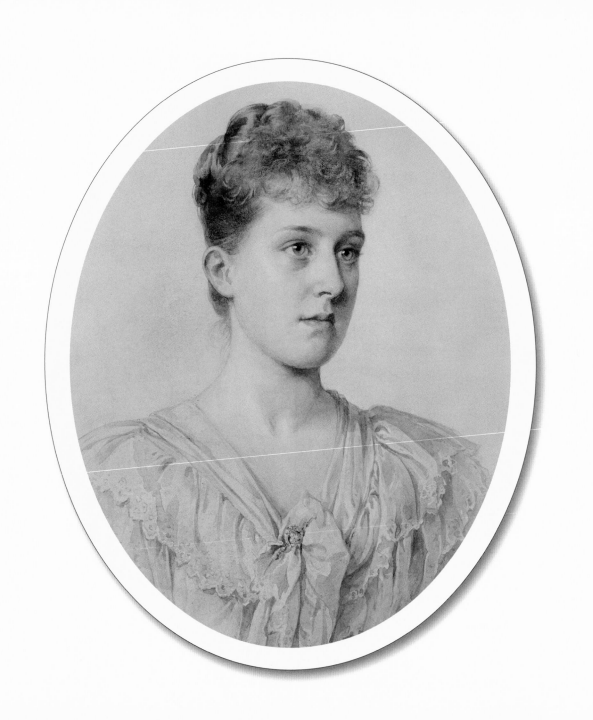

# Introduction

OPPOSITE: Josephine Swoboda, *Princess Marie Louise of Schleswig-Holstein*, 1891. Princess Marie Louise (1872–1956) was the daughter of Queen Victoria's fifth child, Princess Helena, and thereby first cousin to King George V. A childhood friend of Queen Mary, after her unhappy marriage to Prince Aribert of Anhalt was annulled she moved back into Cumberland Lodge in Windsor Great Park (the house that had been her father's home, as Ranger of the Park). It was her popularity in artistic circles that contributed greatly to the success of the Dolls' House. In a letter to his wife, Lutyens described the Princess as being 'full of bounce and fun', and gave her the nickname 'Mary Louse' (while she in turn called him 'Sned').

BELOW: Sir William Rothenstein, *Sir Edwin Lutyens*. The suitability of Sir Edwin Lutyens (1869–1944) – he was knighted in 1918 – as the architect of this 'Palace of Enchantment' was twin-speared: not only had he created a multitude of Arts and Crafts houses so indigenously English that they seem to grow out of the very body of the Surrey landscape and beyond, but he was also responsible for many First World War memorials, most notably the Cenotaph in Whitehall.

It is as extraordinary as it is wonderful that, after the First World War, the great and the good of the largest empire in the world chose to mark the moment by concentrating whatever was finest, most ingenious and most beautiful in the country within the narrow confines of – a dolls' house, albeit one which to this day is considered among the finest architectural models in the world.

How and why did this happen? How was it possible that this little house-within-a-house should ensnare the devotion of over a thousand of the great men and women of the day, as well as three years' passionate attention by the country's greatest architect?

It was Princess Marie Louise, Queen Victoria's granddaughter, who first thought 'on the impulse of the moment' of asking her friend the renowned architect Edwin Lutyens to design a dolls' house for Queen Mary, the consort of Marie Louise's first cousin, King George V. Queen Mary was an obsessive collector of *objets d'art*, most particularly of 'tiny craft', and most passionately of those with a family connection, which she amassed with an acutely knowledgeable eye. There could have been no better gift for her than a dolls' house filled with diminutive treasures. What more suitable tribute, too, could be created for the Queen as a mark of respect

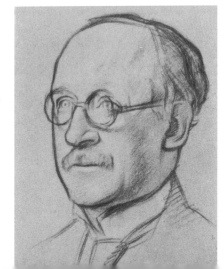

*King George V and Queen Mary in Coronation Robes, 22 June 1911.* Queen Mary's passion for collecting was all-consuming. Having inherited the love of it from her parents, Francis, Prince of Teck and Princess Mary Adelaide, a granddaughter of George III, she was, from the earliest days of her marriage, relentlessly determined to retrieve and reassemble whatever historic royal relics had been scattered throughout the royal households, or had otherwise found their way to the salerooms. Thanks to her, many important pieces were restored and collections brought together again. Happily hand-in-hand with this considerable service went her craving to collect all things small for her own pleasure, which she did with an endless and zestful glee. So it is that every surface in the state rooms of what she often referred to as 'My Dolls' House' displays tiny treasures. In, as she called it, 'My Bedroom', a Fabergé mouse (given by the Grand Duchess Xenia of Russia) sits on her writing table, alongside a miniature of the King.

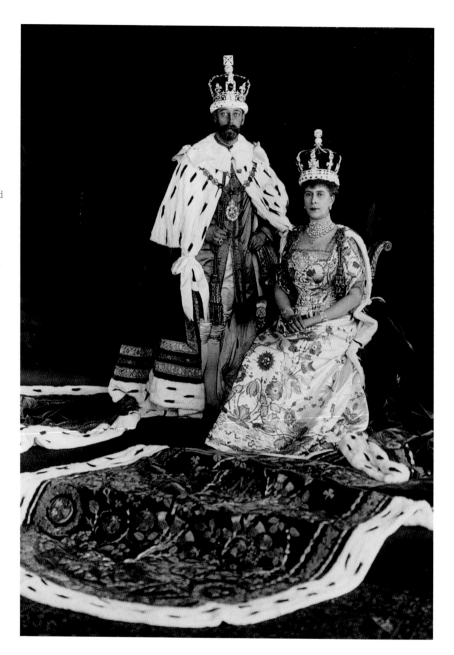

The view through the King's Wardrobe. In this period Lutyens was designing in his 'Wrenaissance' style; his refinement of classicism inspired by the spirit of Inigo Jones and by Christopher Wren, whose influences can be seen whispering through the façades of the little building.

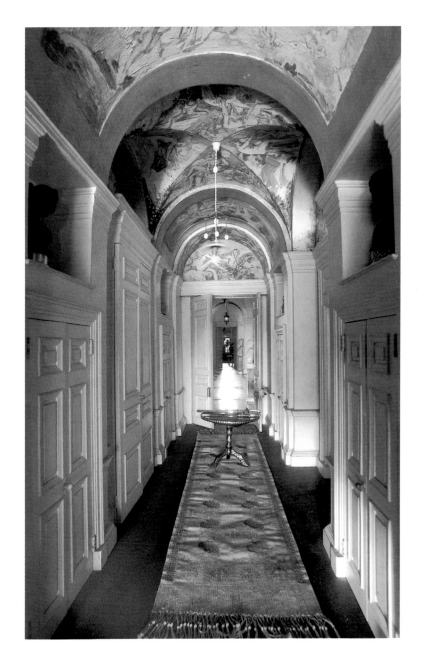

for her steadfast presence throughout the War? With its English eccentricity, this miniature yet monumental scheme was spot-on to capture the world's imagination.

As a last hollering HUZZAH for the vanishing Edwardian age (with loud echoes and overlaps too from the Victorians) the Queen's Dolls' House, which now belongs to Queen Mary's granddaughter, Queen Elizabeth II, is a creation unlike any other. An exquisite little building, designed with serious intent by the great architect of the day and filled to its royal rafters with the work, in miniature, of the finest artists and artisans, craftsmen and manufacturers of early twentieth-century Britain. Such is its sympathy, accuracy and attention to detail that, within seconds of staring into its tiny chambers, all sense of scale is swept away. Roam your eyes through the rooms great and small (the views through the doors are particularly beguiling) and a spell is cast, magically enabling you to feel as if you are strolling through a sensational set-piece, untouched by human hand since the day it was finished in 1924. I rest my case: this is something of a miracle.

*The Book of the Queen's Dolls' House* and *The Book of the Queen's Dolls' House Library*, both published by Methuen and Co. Ltd in 1924, with a selection of miniature volumes from the Library.

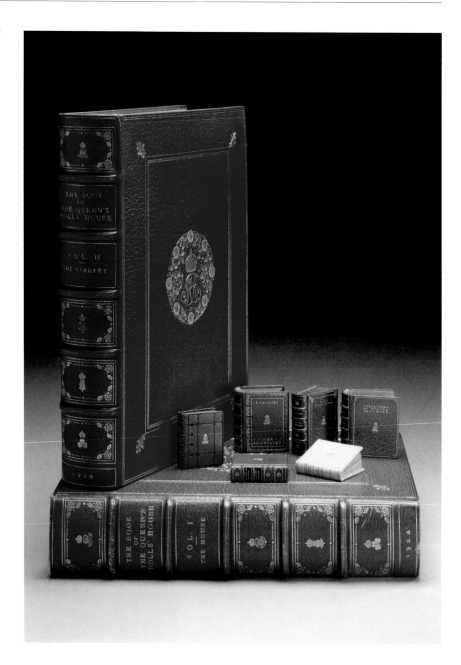

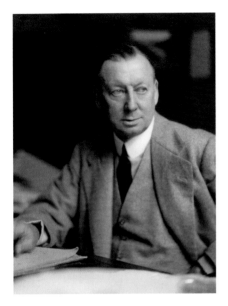

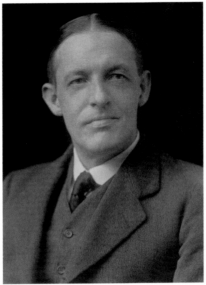

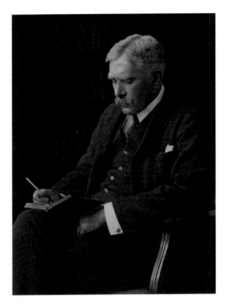

E.V. (Edward Verrell) Lucas (1868–1938) was a highly prolific and popular writer, producing poetry, novels, biography and essays on everything from travel to cricket. A close friend of both Lutyens and Princess Marie Louise, he was instrumental in the assemblage of works for the miniature Library.

The architectural writer Lawrence Weaver (1876–1930) was knighted for his directorship of the United Kingdom stands at the British Empire Exhibition in Wembley, where the Dolls' House was first shown. As architectural editor of *Country Life* he was the ideal individual to involve in the authentic furnishing of the house's interior.

A.C. (Arthur Christopher) Benson (1862–1925), academic and author, is best known today for his words to 'Land of Hope and Glory'. Son of E.W. Benson, Archbishop of Canterbury, he was Master of Magdalene College, Cambridge, at the time of the Dolls' House's production.

In 1924 a limited edition of two official volumes was published: *The Book of the Queen's Dolls' House* and *The Book of the Queen's Doll's House Library*. The first was edited by the essayist and poet A.C. Benson and the architectural writer Sir Lawrence Weaver, the second by popular author E.V. Lucas. Involved at every stage of the Dolls' House's creation, these three marshalled the forces of its most important contemporary chroniclers to write on every aspect of the little building. At the same time the smaller and mainly condensed *Everybody's Book of the Queen's Dolls' House* was published. With the very taste of those times on the tongues of all the contributors, as it were, you will find that they have been quoted in this volume whenever possible.

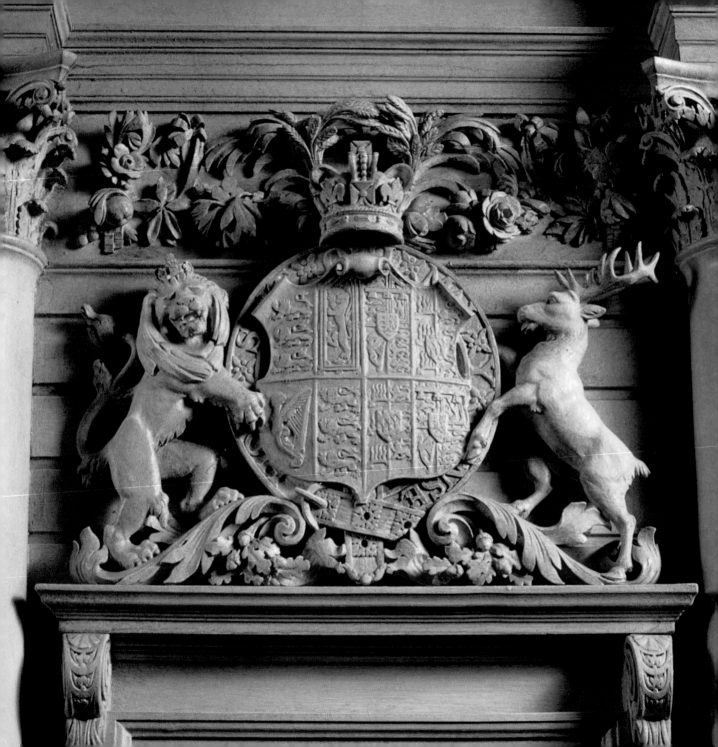

# CHAPTER ONE

# *Architecture and Ornament*

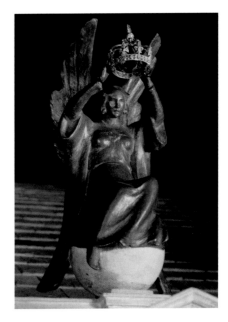

In 1921, when Lutyens took on the Dolls' House, he had been working on the building of New Delhi for nine years; a grand scheme that, with the growth of India's independence movement, was becoming ever more provocatively anachronistic. Changes and cut-backs, for economic reasons, were forever being made to his vast Viceroy's House, and when the chance came to build a full-whack wonder for Queen Mary – albeit in miniature – Lutyens embraced it with gusto. Also hugely important for the architect was that he could design the Dolls' House in the classical style, an ideal that he had been forced to dilute with Indian elements in New Delhi. It gave him particular pleasure to be simultaneously applying himself to eighty square miles of Imperial buildings as well as to a Dolls' House measuring only five feet high. Unbeknown to him, greater glory lay ahead, with the strange scenario of the Queen's Dolls' House becoming a symbol of Britain's post-War renewal.

These were the years of post-War convalescence, when the largely unemployed

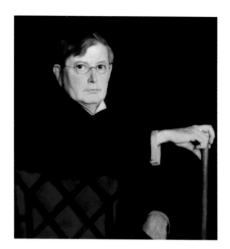

Sir George Frampton (1860–1928) was the sculptor responsible for the House's exterior ornamentation, as well as for the lions at the British Museum and the statue of Peter Pan which stands in Kensington Gardens.

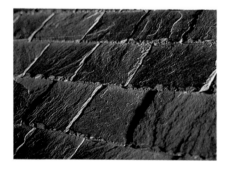

The roof is made up of real slates.

OPPOSITE: The front of the House showing the garden.

country (for architects, artists and craftsmen it was particularly bleak) needed help to stand on its feet once again, in a country 'fit for heroes to live in'. In 1922 the British Empire Exhibition of Arts and Manufacturing, conceived to boost spirits and to stimulate trade, was given the go-ahead; what could be a more cheering centrepiece than this tiny masterpiece model of an English house, displaying the very best that the United Kingdom could offer? So it was that this remarkable creation, which could well have become a mere plaything for Queen Mary's pleasure, a fantastical toy subsumed into the wealth of the Royal Collection, was to become instead a work of art – in fact hundreds of works of art – and a beacon of national importance. Indeed, within days of its inception it was seen as a flagship of endeavour to ease the nation's woes.

'That most frolicsome of men and architects, Sir Edwin Lutyens… at once took fire', wrote E.V. Lucas. 'Everyone to whom he communicated the scheme took fire too.' Lutyens regularly began to hold what he called 'Dolleluiah Dinners', and these were eventually to inspire over 1,500 individuals to become involved in the Dolls' House in one way or another. It was a formidable force, the whole gamut of early 1920s British life (with dashing additions from both India and America): 250 craftsmen and manufacturers, 60 artist-decorators and 700 artists, 600 writers and 500 donors, many of them still household names today. Many too that have long since been forgotten – vanished footprints in the sand, brought into exquisitely sharp focus when seen again in this little building.

Lutyens treated the design of the Dolls' House as an ingenious architectural exercise, whereby (within the strictest rules of symmetry) he created lofty royal chambers along with mezzanine levels, and ensured that every room had a window, with either casement or real sliding sashes, all of them adding to the perfection of the whole. 'It is because the Queen's Dolls' House … shows a just balance between tradition and invention', wrote Sir Lawrence Weaver, 'that it must be regarded not as an architectural whim or as an elaborate nursery jest, but as a serious synthesis of the building arts of our generation.'

Built on the Imperial scale of 1 inch to 1 foot; 5 feet (1.52 m) high, 102 inches (2.59 m) wide, and 58.5 inches (1.49 m) deep, it is almost small enough to give the

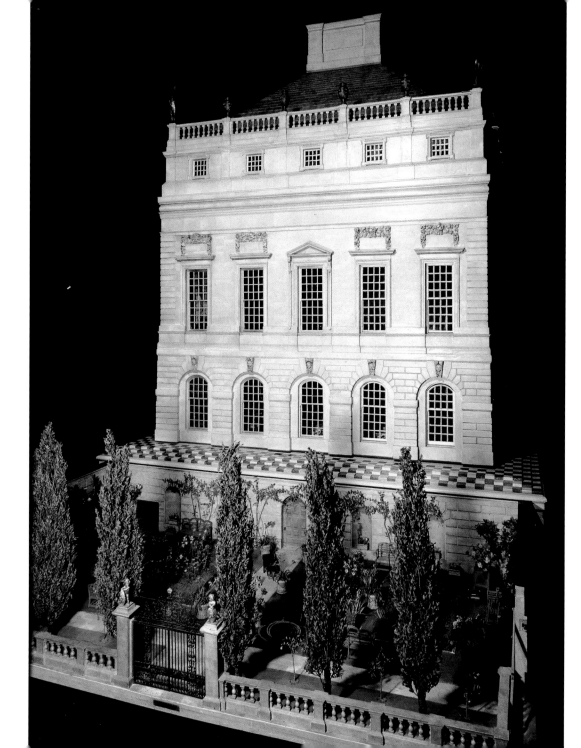

The prams, perambulators, or baby carriages
as they were then called, swaying like deep
black boats suspended on springs, were all made
by Marmet of Letchworth.

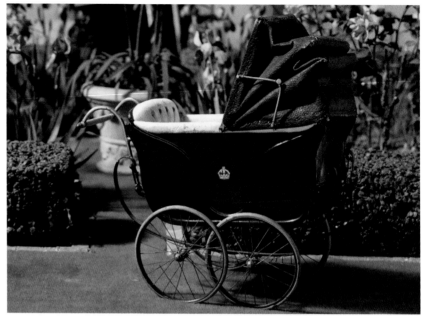

A stone balustrade bulges forth, with wrought-iron
gates and stone piers, bearing lead cherubs holding
the royal arms created by the sculptor Grinling
Gibbons (1648–1721). A cipher of two *G*s
intertwining to form the letter *M*, found at the top
of the gates, also appears embroidered over the
bedhead in the Queen's Bedroom (see p.65).

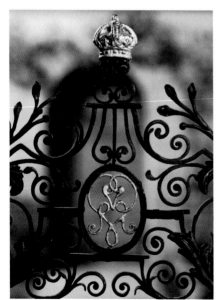

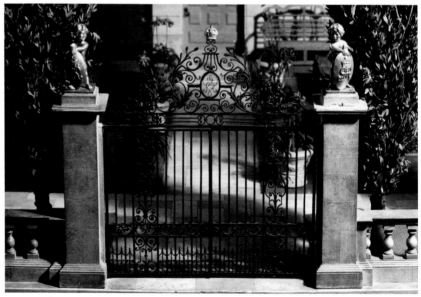

viewer an agreeable sense of being able to embrace it in one satisfying go, and smothering it with admiring kisses.

From the outside, what initially appears to be a podium supporting and uplifting the house is in actual fact the basement quarters, to be shown off by letting down rusticated stone flaps and revealing, to the north, the water tank and machinery for the lifts; to the south, the Wine Cellar and food stores. Most ingenious of all are the revelations to be found in the great drawers at either end of the building. With the flaps pulled down, ABRACADABRA! To the west you haul forth a fully fledged five-bay garage, housing a fleet of royal limousines; while to the east, a garden by Gertrude Jekyll – empress of garden design in her day – literally leaps into life. With an invisible hinge stretching the width of the Garden, all can be folded flat and pushed out of sight. Pull it out again, fold it over, and like a lively cheer for this little horticultural oasis, its six cypress trees – made from real twigs on iron trunks – all stand up straight once again.

So as to be able to exhibit the Dolls' House exterior and interior at once, Lutyens devised the 'highly ingenious electrical contrivance' to lift the outer shell on high, thereby allowing you, in one glorious go, to see every aspect of the little building, both outside and in. What an interior it is too …

There can surely be few more splendid last salvos from Edwardian England than the decoration applied inside the Dolls' House, with its woodwork, plasterwork and damask-hung walls; its superbly imaginative ceiling paintings, many by master craftsmen of the day; as well as the murals by such giants as William Nicholson and Edmund Dulac. There is a wealth of rich-hued marble, too, much of it presented by the Indian Government. In a letter to Princess Marie Louise, Lutyens had wondered whether 'government would allow us to tap maharajahs for Dollyleuyah? 1) Would the Queen mind? 2) Would the Viceroy?' Whatever he eventually did, he must have done it well, for there is Indian marble on the walls, floors, door-cases, dados and ceilings, and most particularly fashioned into fireplaces which then decreed the decorative colour scheme of the rooms.

The shell of the little building was created in 1921 by Lutyens in his Apple Tree Yard office in London, a handy stone's throw from the Royal Academy.

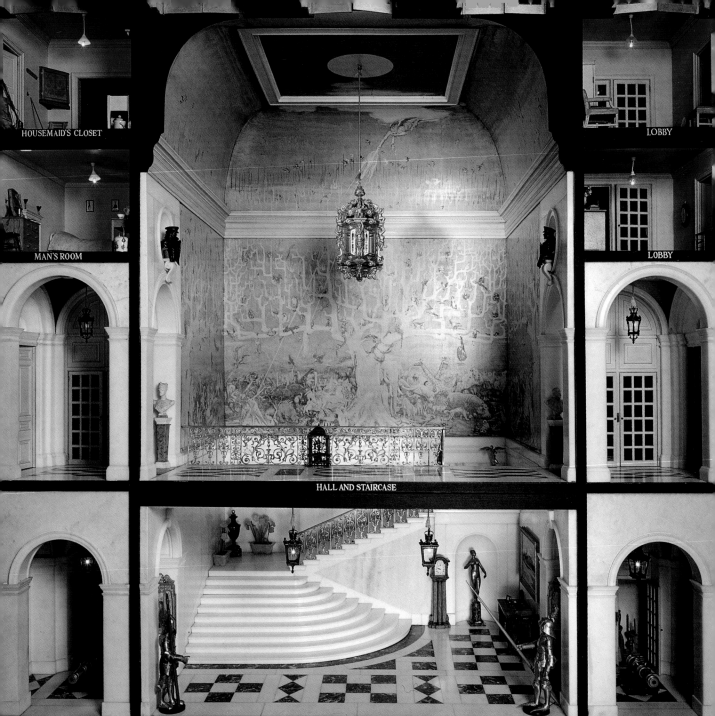

HOUSEMAID'S CLOSET

MAN'S ROOM

LOBBY

LOBBY

HALL AND STAIRCASE

Distinguished Royal Academicians would sally forth to paint the tiny walls and ceilings, often exchanging notes with Queen Mary, who would come to watch their progress. Although Lutyens had the final say, credit must be given to the Queen for delighting for once (her tastes were usually safely conservative) in such avant-garde schemes as the mural for her Bedroom ceiling by Glyn Philpot, with its panel of 'perished mirror work' surrounded by red-winged cherubs amid dark, storm-ridden clouds.

The painted ceilings are the oddest and rarest of all the decorative elements in the house. In the King's Bedroom, the notes of the National Anthem are painted as entwined through canes on a garden gazebo. Naked figures, unmistakably of the 1920s, prance around the cove of the Saloon ceiling, while in panels on high *The Children of Rumour with her Hundred Tongues* veers towards the modernistic. It is a rich roll-call: the Library's sombre beauty of Italian walnut columns and panelling has a painted ceiling by William Walcot (1874–1943), a celebrated architectural draughtsman who left a legacy of buildings in Moscow, while in the Dining Room, ceiling panels and *trompe l'oeil* overdoors were painted by Gerald Moira (1867–1959), a key Pre-Raphaelite figure largely forgotten today but whose work can still be admired in the Old Bailey and the Trocadero Restaurant in London.

All these diverse elements of 1920s England are woven into the very fibre of the house. The culture of the country is embodied in these walls: in the Queen's Bathroom three shallow domes, set in pendentives of smoked snail-shell and painted with mermaids, whales and fish in rippling waves, are all by Maurice Greiffenhagen,

OPPOSITE: The two Halls, with the Grand Staircase – its walls painted by William Nicholson (1872–1949), flanked by servants' quarters.

Close-up of the Queen's Bedroom ceiling by Glyn Philpot (1884–1937). These storm-clouds can perhaps be read as the early shrieks of the artist's torment, torn between devout Catholicism whilst producing establishment art, and his homosexuality and artistic experimentation. The last two won when he and Vivian Forbes – who has a drawing in the Library's folio cabinets – began to live together in 1923.

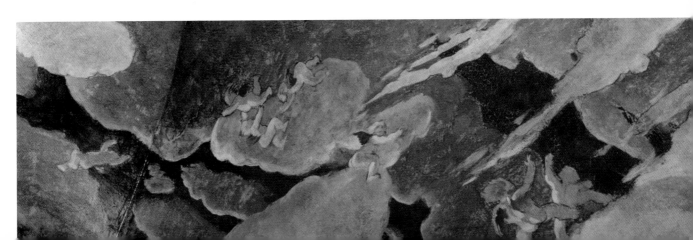

The King's Bedroom ceiling was the work of the
American-born George Plank (1883–1965), a
nationalised Englishman from 1945 who lived
the last years of his life in a house designed for him
by Lutyens. The orange flowers mark the notes for
the tune of the National Anthem.

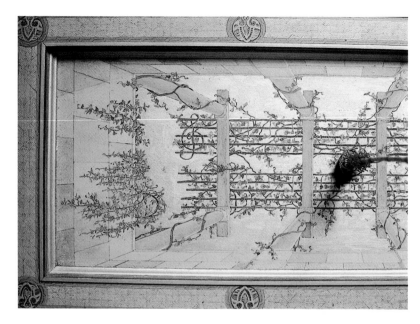

The artist responsible for the decoration of the
Saloon ceiling, Charles Sims (1873–1928), painted
ever more idiosyncratically following his experience
as an official war artist and the death of his son
in the War, and was tragically to drown himself
in the River Tweed.

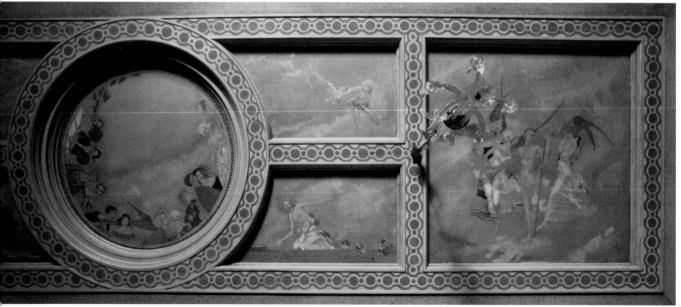

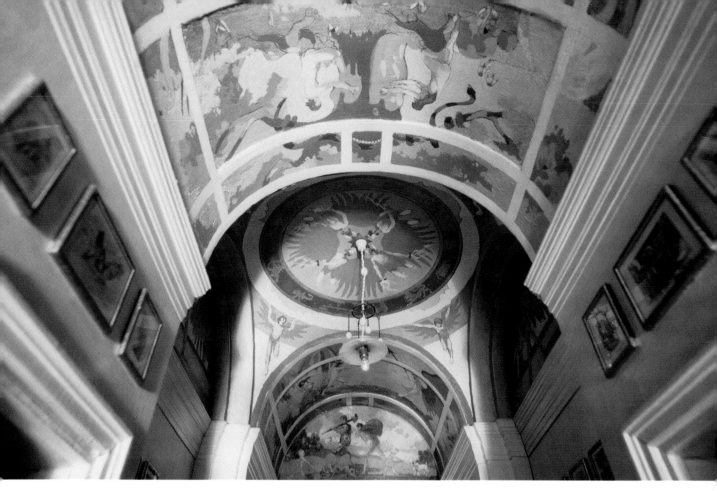

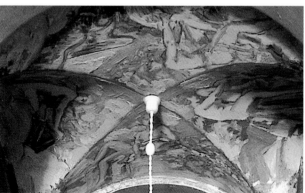

The vaulted ceilings in the King's Bathroom were painted by Captain Laurence Irving (1897–1988) – grandson of the actor Sir Henry Irving.

In the King's Wardrobe (his dressing room) the paintings of writhing naked women are by Wilfrid de Glehn (1870–1951), and give us a glimpse of British Impressionism.

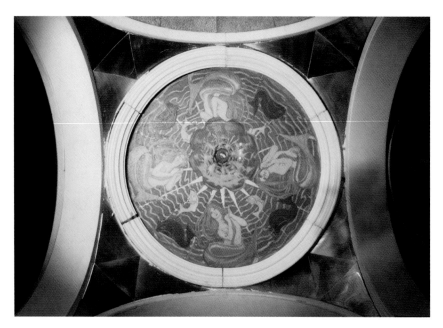

LEFT: The Queen's Bathroom ceiling by
Maurice Greiffenhagen (1862–1931).

BELOW: The Queen's Wardrobe ceiling by
Robert Anning Bell (1863–1933) with its mural
of the senses.

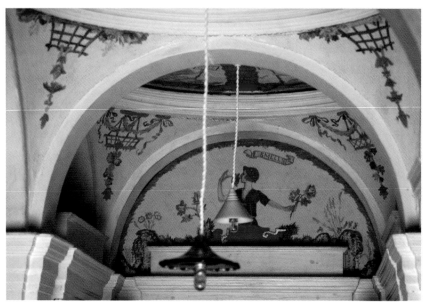

OPPOSITE: William Nicholson, Lutyens' great friend,
was originally asked to paint the coved ceiling in the
Hall. He went the whole hog with a mural over three
floors, of three giant bleached trees soaring over
Adam and Eve as they are expelled from the Garden
of Eden by a winged thunderbolt. They are being
watched, as Nicholson put it, 'by their pets' – which
would appear to be every creature on God's earth.

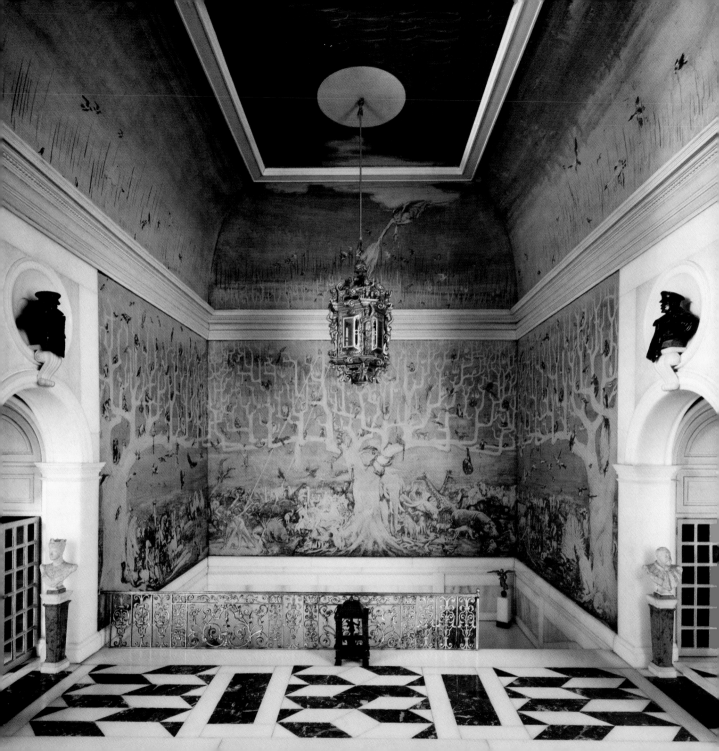

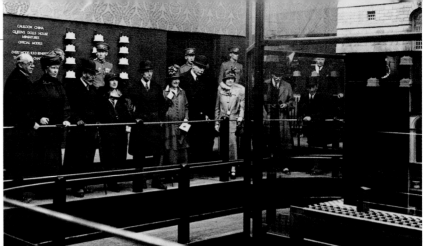

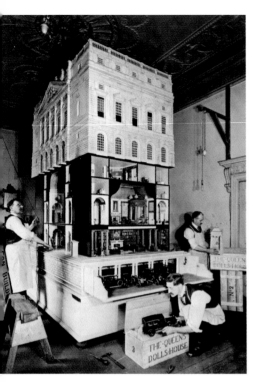

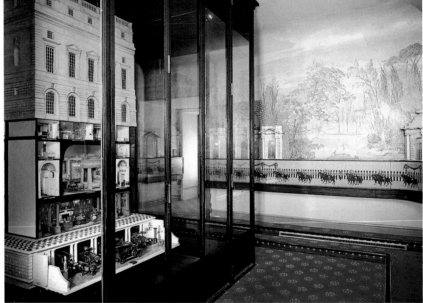

ABOVE: The Dolls' House in Lutyens' home, Mansfield Street.

ABOVE RIGHT: The Dolls' House being admired at the British Empire Exhibition at Wembley by the royal party and Lutyens.

BELOW: The House in its current location at Windsor.

a friend of Rider Haggard and the illustrator of Haggard's popular adventure novel *King Solomon's Mines* (1885). In the Queen's Wardrobe, Robert Anning Bell, a hugely influential artist, illustrator, sculptor and mosaicist, painted circular ceiling panels of the four seasons and the five senses – three of them, strange to see, wearing 1920s' hats.

When the shell of the house was finished (complete with electric wiring and plumbing) it was moved, with the wall of his office being torn down to get it out, to Lutyens' house in Mansfield Street. There it was to stand, taking up half his drawing room for nearly two inconvenient yet wildly exciting years. The elite of the nation's talent had been moved to contribute and they poured through the door: Sir Alfred Munnings (1878–1959) with his miniature painting of Delhi, the King's charger; Alfred Dunhill (1872–1959) with his tiny cigarettes, cigars, pipes and tins of 'My Mixture' – tobacco custom-made for the King. Ursula Ridley, Lutyens' favourite daughter, told me, her eyes alight with delight, of Sir Arthur Conan Doyle (1859–1930) arriving with his diminutive, hand-written and leather-bound story *How Watson Learned the Trick*. Queen Mary, enjoying every development, came to Mansfield Street several times and, according to Lutyens' daughter Mary, her father and the Queen would go for five-mile walks together, exchanging ideas. So great did their friendship become that when the Queen asked the meaning of the *MG* and *GM* embroidered on two tiny pillowcases, Lutyens had no hesitation in explaining saucily: 'May George?' and 'George May'.

In 1924, after three years' work, the Dolls' House was finished. 'The most perfect present that anyone could receive', wrote the Queen to all those involved in its creation. Having been presented to the press – all of them scrunched into the Mansfield Street drawing room – it was borne off to the British Empire Exhibition at Wembley to be shown off in triumph to the nation; although, as was reported in the press 'even dolls' houses… are not immune from the dislocating effects of a general election', political rivalry for centre stage postponing the House's unveiling by a week. During its seven months at Wembley the Dolls' House was to be seen by 1,617,556 people. It was 'A Miracle in Miniature' according to *The Times*, 'a dangerous sight for half-believers in magic'. A year later, to raise money for the Queen's charitable fund, it was taken off again, in forty-five boxes weighing four and a half tons, to the Ideal Home Exhibition at Olympia in West Kensington. Finally, in July 1925, it was put on show in Windsor, in a room specially designed by Lutyens. There it has remained ever since.

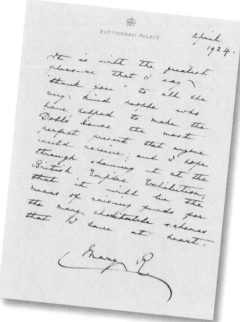

ABOVE: The Queen's letter of thanks 'to all the very kind people who have helped to make the Dolls' House the most perfect present that anyone could receive'.

BELOW: Smoking items, including 'My Mixture', tobacco custom-made for the King.

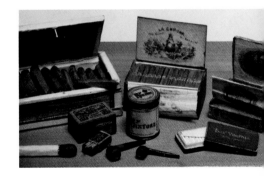

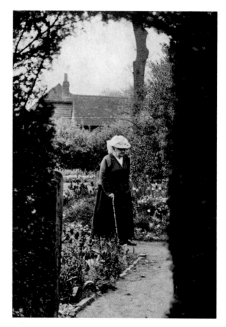

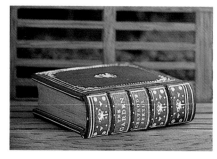

TOP: Gertrude Jekyll (1843–1932) oversaw the creation of the miniature garden.

ABOVE: *The Book of the Garden*, on a bench.

RIGHT: Lutyens' now famed-the-world-over garden benches stand proud, while hydrangeas and rhododendrons are planted in his still-popular wooden tubs.

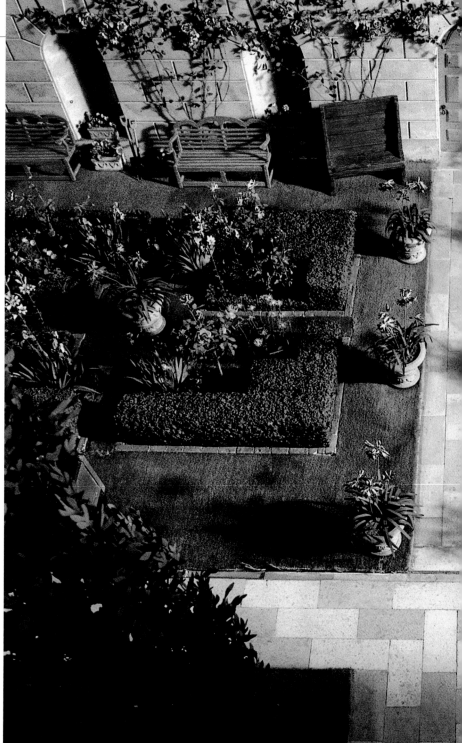

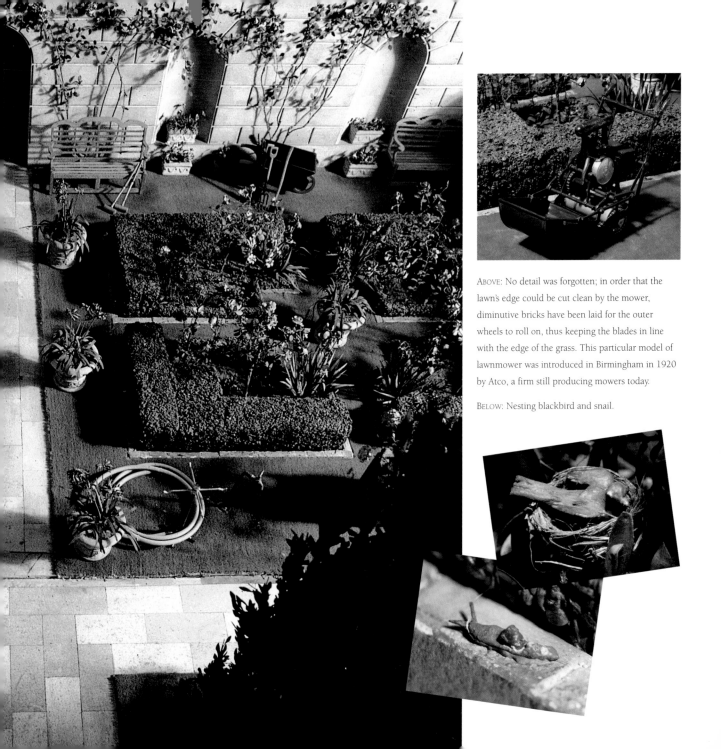

ABOVE: No detail was forgotten; in order that the lawn's edge could be cut clean by the mower, diminutive bricks have been laid for the outer wheels to roll on, thus keeping the blades in line with the edge of the grass. This particular model of lawnmower was introduced in Birmingham in 1920 by Atco, a firm still producing mowers today.

BELOW: Nesting blackbird and snail.

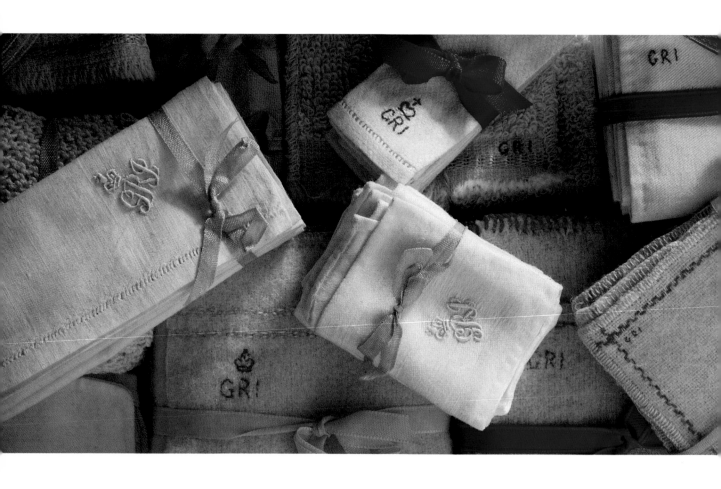

CHAPTER TWO

# Below Stairs

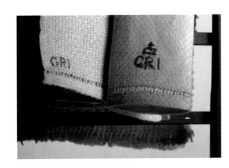

*A further purpose in the minds of those who designed, constructed and furnished the Queen's Dolls' House was to present to Her Majesty a little model of a house of the twentieth century which should be fitted up with perfect fidelity, down to the smallest details so as to represent as closely and minutely as possible a genuine and complete example of a domestic interior with all the household arrangements characteristic of the daily life of the present time ... an interesting and lifelike memorial for future times of the sort of way in which people of our own days found it desirable and agreeable to live ...*

A.C. Benson

*The Book of the Queen's Dolls' House,* 1924

OPPOSITE AND ABOVE: The linen truly astounds, with an abundance of damask, cotton, flannel and wool, from the finest tablecloths to pudding cloths. There are 'royal' sheets, while the servants' pillowcases have buttons barely visible to the naked eye. Red and white glass cloths are stacked beside kitchen roller towels; doilies (round and square) keep company with embroidered napkins. All are neatly stored in the cupboards and tied with coloured ribbons to show where in the house they belong. Every last one is monogrammed with such delicacy that one is tempted to say it could only have been the work of fairies, although in fact it is known to have been done by a lone Irish-French seamstress who spent 1,500 hours on the job.

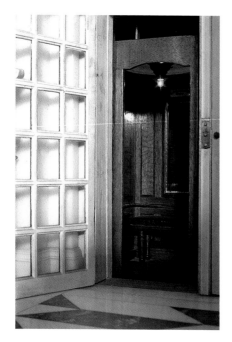

The fully-functioning passenger lift, which is to be found to one side of the Halls.

A photo of Queen Mary in one of the servants' rooms.

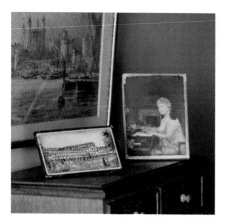

Suppose that a Saxon manor were to be discovered today with every domestic detail intact, or an Elizabethan mansion, or an eighteenth-century stately pile. Being able to see such aspects of daily life would be nothing short of miraculous. Yet that is precisely what can be relished with the Queen's Dolls' House. Here is a unique chance to see the workings of a grand early twentieth-century house, down to its last and most domestic detail.

The Queen's Dolls' House was already somewhat anachronistic when it was built in 1923. In spite of the post-War hard times, Lutyens and his team of creators and contributors still took it for granted that a great house would march forth into the future with an active and hierarchically ranked army of servants. Likewise, the seductive echoes can be heard of Edwardian opulence; echoes that still reverberate through its tiny rooms today. Nor are the servant's quarters forgotten. Here, too, Lutyens characteristically applied himself down to the most diminutive detail, so as to make the lives of their imaginary inhabitants as comfortable as possible (though the lack of a Servants' Hall for convivial get-togethers is regrettable). With the heartbeat of the house thumping away in the Kitchen, the quiet dignity of the wood-lined Linen Room, the whirl of work in various domestic offices, the well-furnished and picture-hung 'Men's' and maids' bedrooms, and the startlingly opulent contents of the Garage, there were separate little kingdoms within this royal household. And with such technological triumphs as five bathrooms (all with running water), two Waygood Otis electric lifts from America (one a 'passenger car' of polished mahogany, the other a 'service car' of polished oak) which with a press of a button fly up and down on finest fishing lines – not forgetting the vast array of up-to-the-minute household aids – life below stairs was not half bad.

With all their domestic paraphernalia intact, these quarters of the Dolls' House are perhaps the most bewitching of all. They include such heart-stirring sights as the framed photograph of a 'Tommy' (it was after all only five years since the end of the War) in every maid's bedroom, as well as alluring actresses for the 'Men', and of course the obligatory portrait of the King or the Queen – all piercing-through-to-your-heart evocations of the period.

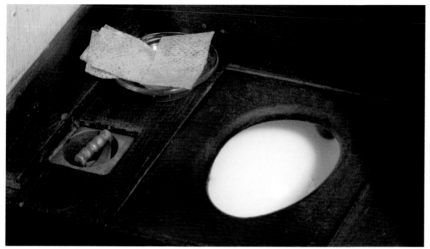

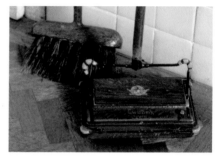

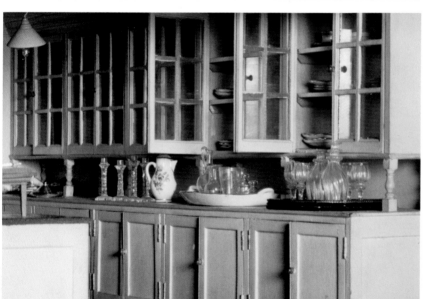

ABOVE LEFT: American 'Bromo' lavatory paper, here pictured with the King's W. C.

ABOVE: The Ewbank Carpet Sweeper, here shown actual size, sits in the Kitchen.

LEFT: The Butler's Pantry.

RIGHT: Sweeps of wooden plate racks in the Butler's Pantry, able to hold ninety plates, marching above the deep lead-lined sinks are especially pleasing.

FAR RIGHT: The Hoover in the Housemaid's Closet.

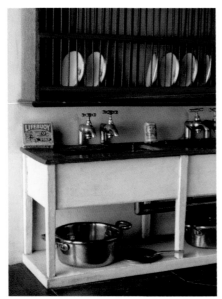

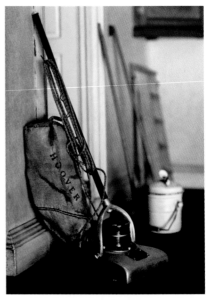

BELOW RIGHT: Cleaning products in the Housemaid's Closet.

BELOW: All these rooms are served with hot and cold running water from sturdy steel taps, although the royal quarters had silver, adding yet more shine to their two beautiful bathrooms.

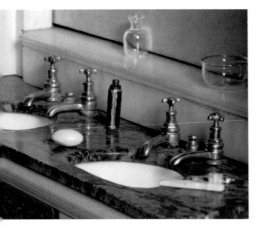

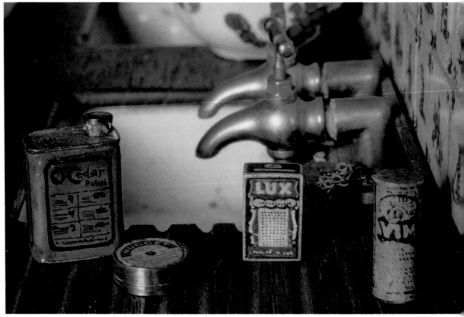

In the working rooms below stairs, too, many of us will have the happiest march down memory lane, entranced by such sights as the wooden Ewbank Carpet Sweeper, produced between 1910 and 1939, with its cord and rubber corner buffers. As for the unyieldingly sharp and shiny lavatory paper, watermarked 'Bromo' on every sheet – these details afford the oddest little glimpses into the past. With the damp cleanliness of scrubbed draining-boards in the Butler's Pantry, the asphyxiating aromas of Lux Flakes, Sunlight Soap and Vim, O'Cedar Polish and Gospo in the Housemaid's Closet, the block of Lifebuoy soap and the enamel slop bucket on the slate-floored scullery, it seems as if the air that you are breathing is that of 1924, forever trapped within these little walls.

'If we suppose that the present Queen's [Dolls'] House lasts on for, say, two hundred years', wrote A.C. Benson, 'the little mansion which seems positively the last word in convenience and beauty … we may be sure that our successors will look at it in astonishment, and wonder that men could ever have deigned to live in so laborious and cumbrous a way … But at the same time, how they will value the house as an historical document!'

There are many reminders of that 'cumbrous' way: for example, the red cone Minimax Fire Extinguisher – 'Minimum effort, Maximum strength' – invented in Germany in 1902 and established in Britain in 1903; then there is a rather lumpen Hoover – one of the Dolls' House's trail-blazing American imports, which was invented by an Ohio janitor in 1902. The cocktail shaker – one of them awaits use in the Service corridor outside the Kitchen – was also from the United States, gaining popularity there in the late 1800s.

## The Kitchen

On the south front, wide and welcoming, the Kitchen rules the domestic roost. With its wood-block floor this was 'no painted pretence', in the words of Sir Lawrence Weaver, who was in charge of showing off the Dolls' House at the Empire Exhibition, 'but two thousand [there are in fact 2,500] tiny sections of veritable oak … Here indeed is a paradise for cooks.' Taking centre stage is Lutyens'

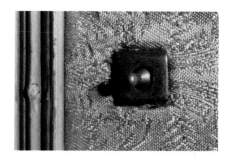

All the lights, however modest, were created with Lutyens' instantly recognisable genius, and all his switches in the house, minute and well-rounded, are of brass.

OVERLEAF: The Kitchen. 'Over all this perfection electric light reigns', wrote Dymphna Ellis – the Kitchen's official chronicler-in-chief, who, providing yet another piece in this great jigsaw of British life, was one of the children photographed by Lewis Carroll in the 1860s – 'and from real glass bulbs, like smallest drops of dew, real light is turned on by real switches.'

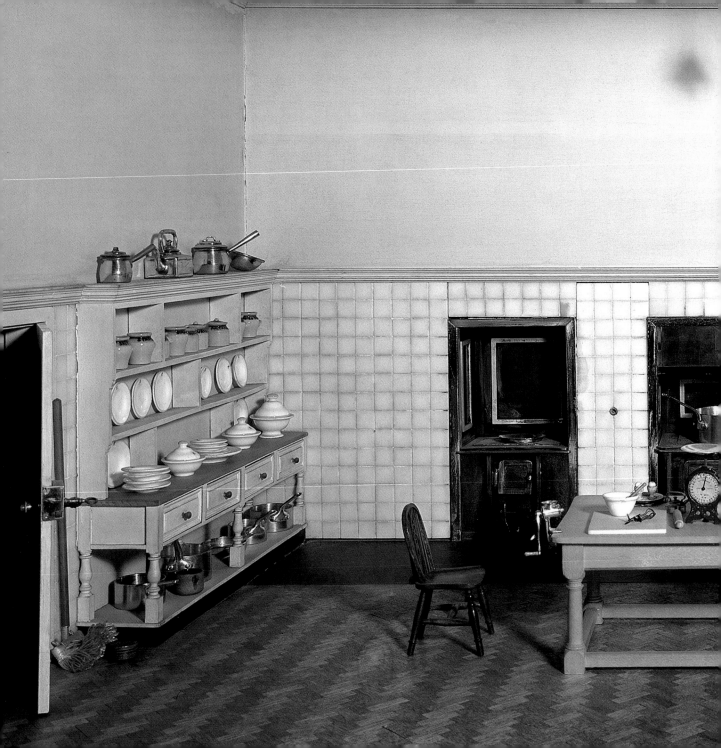

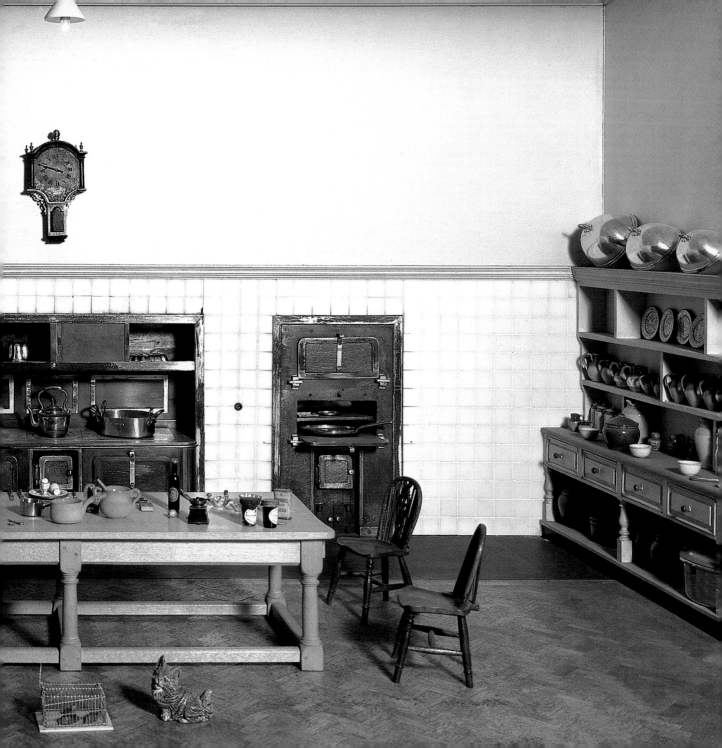

RIGHT: With the usual unerring accuracy of Dolls' House design, the floor along the front of this 'English Range' has been paved with slate.

BELOW: The copper kettle, forever primed for boiling on the hob, was made from a George V penny, and has the King's head, encircled like a miniature, on the base.

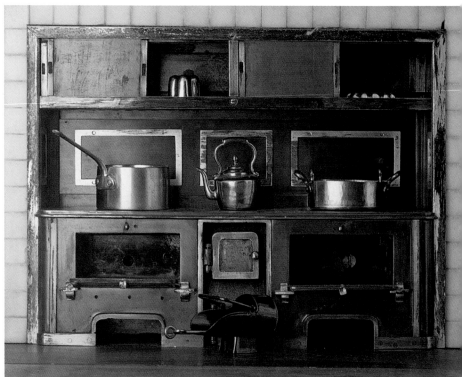

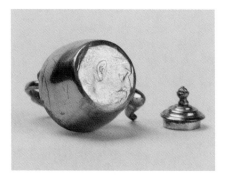

RIGHT: The pots and pans shine like gold, and the model 'bain-marie' is 'the prettiest thing in the world', in the words of Dymphna Ellis. They shine like gold because, most marvellous to write, they are made of gold, hammered into their dainty existence (to avoid future polishing) by the mechanics of Guy's Hospital.

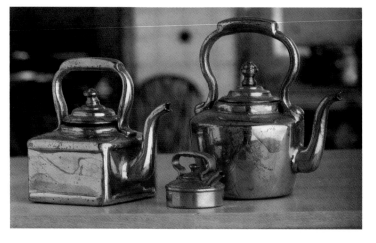

oak table: 'a symbol of the British constitution … and contains that council of perfection, a drawer at each end!' enthused Dymphna Ellis, recorder of the Kitchen and stores. A miniature masterpiece by Lutyens, this is identical to one he designed for his own dining room in London.

Lutyens' gilded and painted-with-cabbage-roses clock hangs high over the polished steel range, which has smaller and separate ovens on either side; one for heating plates, the other for pastry. All three are as handsome as can be, with 'no theatrical display of electricity', wrote Miss Ellis, 'but good honest British coal producing the good old British smoke, truly described by some far-seeing mind as "the source of Britain's greatness".' And like a guard of honour for the old days, a complete copper *batterie de cuisine*, with correctly tinned interiors, stands proud on the dressers.

Today it is as much of a delight to be able to see all these old household pals as it is to dwell on the minds of those who made them. Many have made it triumphantly through to the present day: a tin of Colman's Mustard stands on the Kitchen table – first produced in 1814, it still holds the Royal Warrant granted in 1866; Tiptree jam has been on the go since 1885; Frank Cooper marmalade, founded in 1874, is still a holder of the Royal Warrant; while Lea & Perrins Worcestershire Sauce was established in 1836. There are many more, still going strong, contents and packaging almost unchanged since the day they were put in the Dolls' House Kitchen, nearly a century ago.

Agnes Jekyll (1861–1937) – sister of Gertrude, who designed the Dolls' House Garden – was in charge of the Kitchen stores. Ever sensitive to the trouble that might be created by choosing one firm over another, she wrote to Princess Marie Louise that they would have 'to do this with some caution so as not to give cause for offence or jealousy … I think it will be well to send the letters to such firms as already supply the Royal Household, or those who are specially eminent in their productions. Space will be limited … but if Huntley and Palmer contribute, Peek and Frean … may be embittered at being excluded. If we suggested

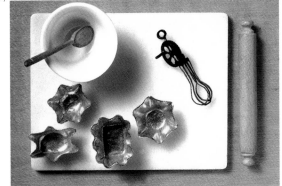

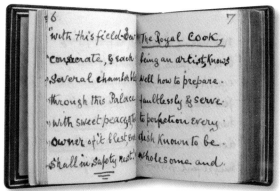

Top: Pastry moulds, rolling pin and board.

Above: *The Dolls' House Cookery Book*, by Agnes Jekyll.

RIGHT: There are singular stars in this culinary extravaganza which send you spiralling back in time; none more so than the great round wooden knife machine – 'Kent's Patent 199 High Holborn, London' of 1870 – designed to clean steel knives but already old-fashioned by 1924, by which date stainless steel cutlery was in widespread use. Up to twelve knives could be dealt with at a time, pushed into slots and cleaned and polished by leather blades, felt pads and bristles. Whilst pouring abrasive emery powder into the drum, you crank the handle round, often with the dire result of wearing the blades to razor-blade thinness.

ABOVE FAR RIGHT: There is also a wood-handled coffee grinder, which can be scrunched into life; with a base only 1 cm square, it was described by our poetic Miss Ellis as being 'a gem of the rarest water' with the drawer for the grounds having 'the smallest knob in the whole establishment or indeed, I venture to say, in the whole world!' Its actual size is shown in silhouette below.

BELOW RIGHT: Recently and surprisingly, the 'labour-saving' Besco Brush Mop – patented in 1923 – has been discovered to have a name plate of pure gold; a right royal exception to the usual brass.

BELOW FAR RIGHT: Weighing scales.

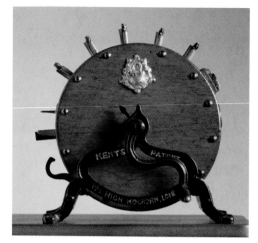

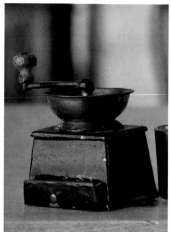

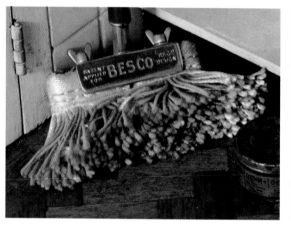

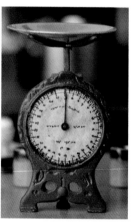

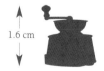

1.6 cm

tea from Twining, some of the other great Tea houses, The Indian Tea-growers and the Ceylon Tea Association, may complain.' As well as picking her way through this minefield of good manners, Agnes Jekyll also wrote *The Dolls' House Cookery Book* for the Library. 'The Royal Cook,' she wrote, 'being an artist, knows well how to prepare faultlessly & serve to perfection every dish known to be wholesome and nourishing, and pleasant both to the palate and to the eye.' For breakfast she recommended brioches with cups of frothed chocolate, and a touch of whipped cream; for 'a festive tea party' she proposed a Chelsea bun as well as a Russian ice of blackcurrant leaves. Pleasing proof of her influence is to be seen in the large Chinese jar for lavender, for which she had the following aromatic suggestion: 'To sweeten the atmosphere before the guests assemble, and after savoury dishes have been prepared. Heat a shovel, or any such metal surface, very hot, and strew on it dried heads of lavender; the air will soon smell deliciously of that fragrant plant.' Last but not least in this engine room of the Dolls' House, three ivory mice in a humane mouse-trap are forever desired by a crystal cat.

## The Linen Room

'The store of linen might gladden any housewife's heart', wrote A.C. Benson. So it most certainly should, with its cupboard-lined room – 31½ feet (9.6m) long in human scale – placed right in the centre of the top floor, thus giving the royal housekeeper her rightful role in the hierarchy of the house. Doubling as her sitting room – in which that most reactionary of newspapers *The Morning Post* is on hand to read – it is a particularly soothing spot, with a hand-woven Chinese carpet, marble fireplace and iron hob grate.

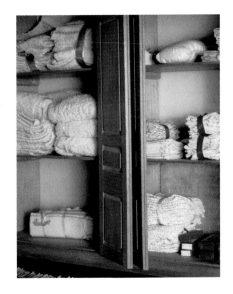

ABOVE: This quantity of linen was deemed essential, allowing every item to 'rest' between laundering and use.

BELOW: The Linen Room.

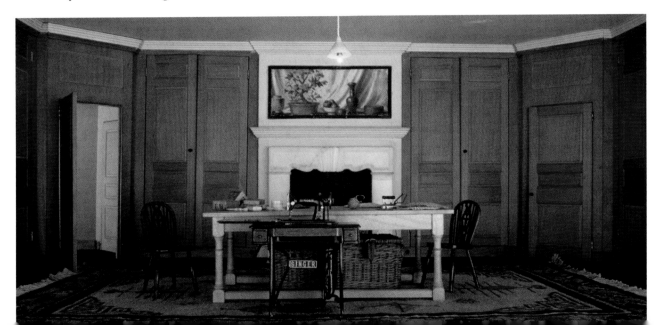

RIGHT: Here again, America has marched to England's aid, with the treadle Singer Sewing Machine. Invented by Isaac Merritt Singer in 1850, here it is, in all its silvered, gilded and mahogany glory.

INSET: The electric iron too stands proud, having crossed the Atlantic after it was invented by Henry W. Seely in New York in 1882.

BELOW LEFT: The supplies of Clark's Cotton – wrapped in blue embossed tissue paper within their blue boxes – came from Paisley in Scotland.

BELOW RIGHT: Wicker hampers – so large when life-size as to have to be carried by two men – stand ready for the laundry.

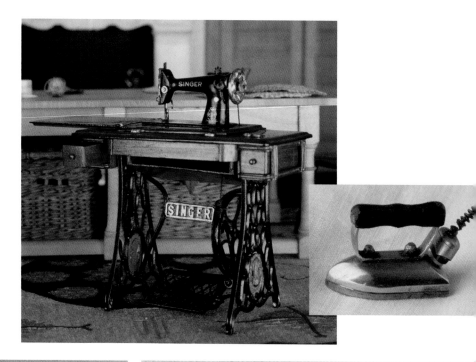

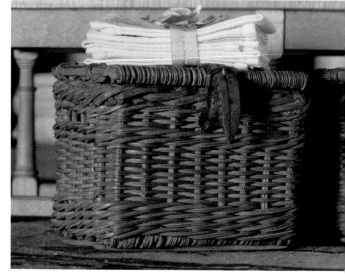

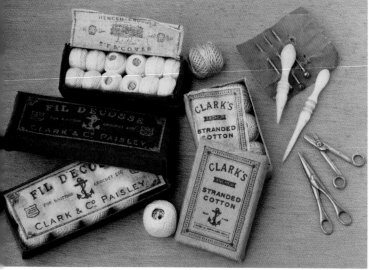

## The Servants' Quarters

Adjoining her linen kingdom, the Housekeeper's Bedroom is furnished with an importance equal only to the Butler's. It is the very ordinariness of these rooms that makes them so special in their survival – few, if any, such authentic rooms are left in the land today. They show us such long-lost sights as stern iron bedsteads with flock mattresses on wire springs, along with military brushes and Odontasse toothpaste, bottles of Eno's Fruit Salts (invented in Newcastle in the 1850s by James Crossley Eno) as well as razors less than ½ inch (1.2 cm) long. And chamber pots are to be found under every bed.

The Housekeeper's Room.

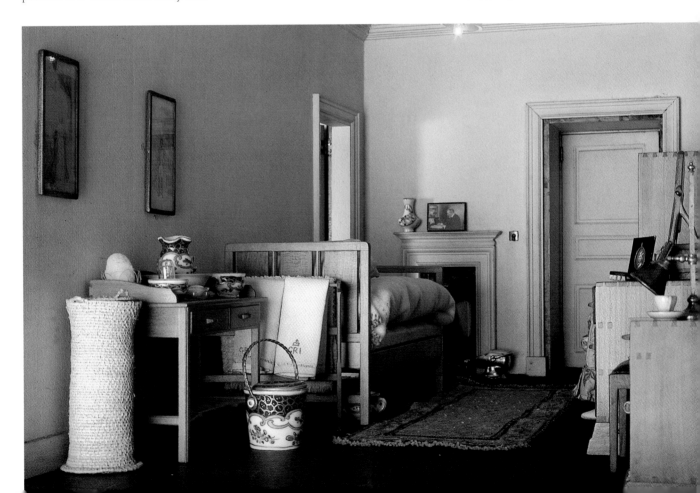

RIGHT: A servant's bed with mattress.

FAR RIGHT: Much of the furniture, including the
men's trouser presses, was made by Waring and
Gillow. Founded in 1897, after the merger of Gillow
of Lancaster and Waring of Liverpool, this firm was
so popular with the swells that it was parodied in
Gilbert and Sullivan's *HMS Pinafore*:

> On the one hand, papa's luxurious home
> Hung with ancestral armour and old brasses
> Carved oak and tapestry from distant Rome
> Rare 'blue and white' Venetian finger-glasses
> Rich oriental rugs, luxurious sofa pillows
> And everything that isn't old, from Gillows.

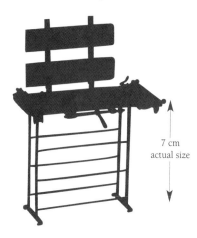

7 cm
actual size

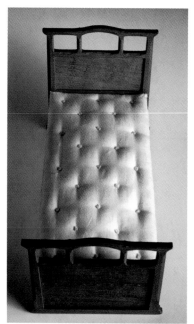

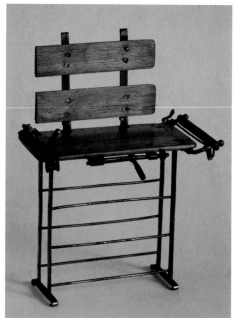

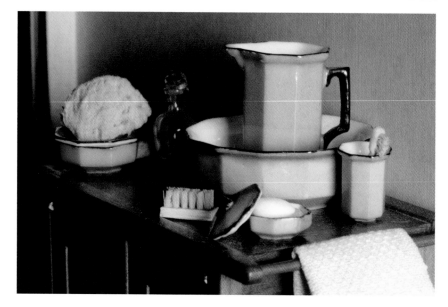

All the staff bedrooms have variations of the same
Cauldron Pottery washstand sets – wash bowl, jug,
tooth mug, slop bucket and sponge and soap bowls
– complete with an Allen and Hanburys sponge
and Pears soap. The Butler's set (pictured here)
is the same as the Princess Royal's.

All the men's bedrooms have trouser presses. These, and much of the other furniture – wood, good and solid – was made by the great firm of Waring and Gillow, with holly-wood beds and horsehair mattresses for the more senior staff, and the Butler being honoured with a fine suite in unstained cherry-wood, designed by Lutyens himself.

The paintings, drawings and prints for these rooms, often by artists of note, were obviously given careful consideration; none more so than the powerful First World War painting *Bringing up the Guns* by the equestrian artist Lucy Kemp-Welch, hung on the walls for 'Man Number 4'. The Butler was favoured with a landscape by the painter-poet Adrian Stokes, whose work also hangs in the King's Bedroom. Paintings of Edinburgh Castle by Frank Moss Bennett (1874–1952) in 'Maid's Bedroom Number 3', as well as his *Tower of London* in 'Man's Bedroom Number 4' are happily a world away from his usual genre paintings of cardinals, huntsmen and bewigged heroes; hugely popular in the 1920s, these have now thankfully vanished with barely a trace.

Such details constantly flummox you into thinking this must be a real house. With a fire in every servant's bedroom – albeit having to be lit, along with all the others in the House, by the maids in the early hours of the morning – these would have been cosy quarters. Reading material for the servants took the form of *Country Life*, as well as the highbrow *Pearson's Magazine*, which in 1922 was the first in the country to publish a crossword puzzle.

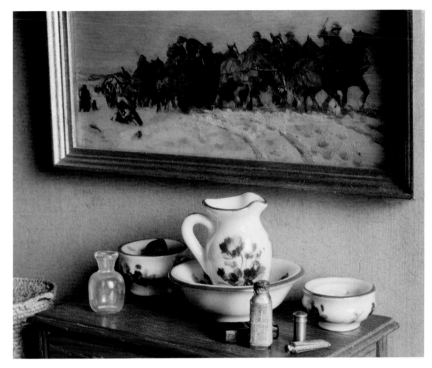

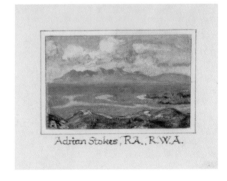

TOP: *Bringing Up the Guns* by Lucy Kemp-Welch (1869–1958), hanging in the bedroom of Man Number 4.

ABOVE: *Landscape* by Adrian Stokes (1854–1935).

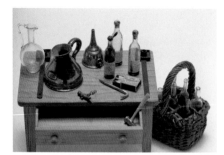

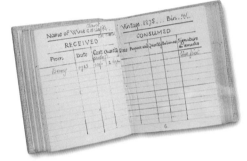

Top: The Wine Cellar would have been the Butler's domain. All the impedimenta required for such duties as decanting here await him.

Above: Another important daily duty would have been to keep the Cellar Book in order. Under columns of Received and Consumed, this little volume records that in 1923 two dozen bottles of Château Lafite 1875 were bought from Berry Bros for 200 shillings a dozen.

Right: The Wine Cellar.

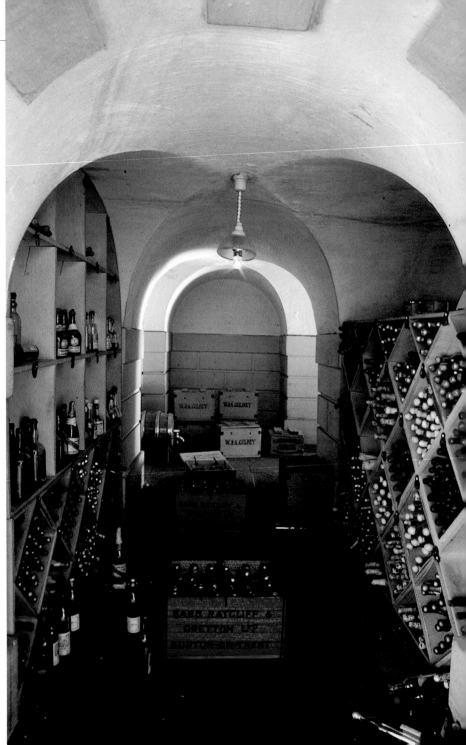

## The Cellars

For those who delight in such domestic details, what is to be found in the Cellars will set them hollering with joy. Descending steep stairs, into nine dimly lit groin-vaulted corridors of rusticated 'stone' (as with the exterior, in fact painted wood), is to be submerged yet again in the very essence of the age. In the Dry Goods Store, so ample, according to A.C. Benson, 'that the house could be victualled to last out a moderate siege', memories are stacked high alongside bottles of 'Bull's Eyes' and 'Barley Sugar'. Your taste buds tingle too with 'Maltex … Invigorating and Nutritional'.

The Wine Cellar is another sight for sore eyes with its one hundred dozen bottles of the finest champagnes, wines and spirits and beers; all laid down in their wooden honeycomb compartments and on the shelves of their noble vaulted quarters. They were chosen with all the care and expertise worthy of the Royal Household by Francis Berry, senior partner of Berry Bros of St James's Street in London, a firm founded in 1699 and today Britain's oldest wine and spirits merchant. Although somewhat evaporated, they could even today be ecstatically tasted on the tip of the tongue.

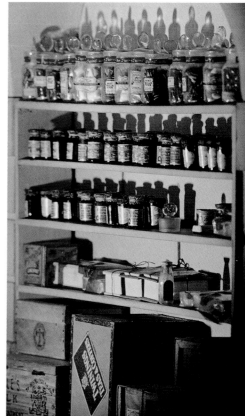

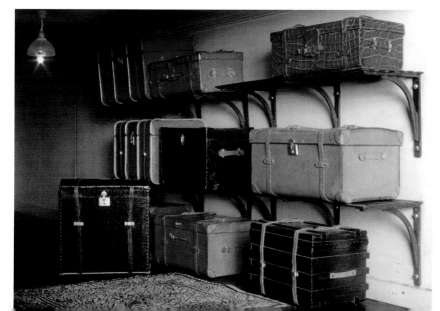

ABOVE: The Dry Goods Store.

LEFT: The Trunk Room throws up yet more memories, with its assembly of luggage in pigskin, snakeskin and crocodile, as well as tin and even wood. There are portmanteaux, as well as hat, boot and book boxes, a 'Mannequin Box' and tube for umbrellas.

## Inventory of the Wine Cellar

| QUANTITY | VINTAGE |
|---|---|
| *Champagne* | |
| 5 dozen | Veuve Clicquot 1906 |
| 5 dozen | Pommery & Greno 1915 |
| 5 dozen | Louis Roederer 1911 |
| 5 dozen | G.H. Mumm & Co. 1911 |
| 2 dozen | G.H. Mumm & Co. 1911 (magnums) |
| | |
| *Claret* | |
| 2 dozen | Château Lafite, Grand Vin 1875 |
| 2 dozen | Ch. Haut-Brion 1888 |
| 2 dozen | Château Margaux 1899 |
| 2 dozen | Ch. Le Prieuré 1918 |
| | |
| *Port* | |
| 2 dozen | Cockburn Smithes & Co.1878 |
| 2 dozen | Taylor Fladgate 1896 |
| 2 dozen | Warre 1900 |
| 2 dozen | Fonseca 1908 |
| 2 dozen | Dow 1912 (magnums) |
| 2 dozen | Royal Tawny |

| | |
|---|---|
| *Sherry* | |
| 2 dozen | Amoroso Pale Golden |
| 2 dozen | Oloroso Puro 1872 |
| | |
| *Madeira* | |
| 2 dozen | Finest Bual 1820 |
| 2 dozen | Chablis-Moutonne 1904 |
| | |
| *White Burgundy* | |
| 2 dozen | Montrachet 1889 |
| 2 dozen | Graves-Supérieur |
| | |
| *Sauternes* | |
| 2 dozen | Château Yquem 1874 |
| | |
| *Burgundy* | |
| 2 dozen | Romanée 1904 |
| | |
| *Hock* | |
| 2 dozen | Rudesheimer |

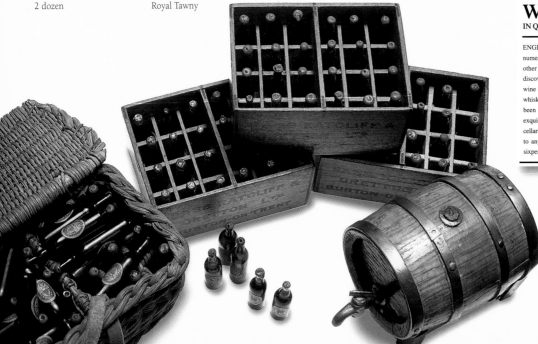

# DRYS PROTEST WINE CELLARS
### IN QUEEN MARY'S DOLLHOUSE, LONDON

ENGLISH PROHIBITIONISTS, who, although not numerous, are as decided in their views as those of any other land, have been aroused to indignation by the discovery that Queen Mary's million-dollar dollhouse has wine cellars containing miniature cases of champagne, whiskey and other alcoholic beverages ... Protests have been made but without results and Her Majesty's exquisitely furnished replica of a fine English home, wine cellars and all, will be on show at the Wembley Exhibition, to any and all of her subjects who wish to contribute sixpence to charity.

Extract from the *New York Times*,
14th April 1924.

*French Vermouth*

| | |
|---|---|
| 2 dozen | Noilly Prat (litres) |

*Italian Vermouth*

| | |
|---|---|
| 2 dozen | Martini Rossi |

*Spirits*

| | |
|---|---|
| 2 dozen | Grande Fine Champagne Brandy 1854 |
| 1 dozen | Hennessy's Brandy |
| 2 dozen | Dry London Gin |
| 1 dozen | Fine Old Jamaica Rum |

*Scotch Whisky*  ¼ cask 28 gallons G. & J.G. Smith's Glenlivet 1910

*Irish Whisky*  J. Jameson & Sons, Dublin 1907

Also, 1 dozen of each of the following, all 'bottled' by Berry Bros & Co.
Pères Chartreux Litres Yellow
Benedictine, D.O.M.
Riga Kummel, Fleur de Cumin
Sloe Gin
Cherry Brandy
Apricot Liqueur
Crème de Menthe, Cusenier

And:

| | |
|---|---|
| 1 dozen | Gilbey's Champagne Brandy |
| 1 dozen | Gilbey's Whisky |
| 2 dozen | Gilbey's Tawny Port |
| 1 dozen | Château Laudenne |
| 1 dozen | Vintage Claret |
| 12 dozen | Bass' Pale Ale |
| 5 dozen | Bass' King's Ale |
| 2 casks | Bass' Pale Ale |
| 2 cases | Gordon & Tanqueray's London Gin |
| 1 dozen cases | 'Johnnie Walker' Whisky |

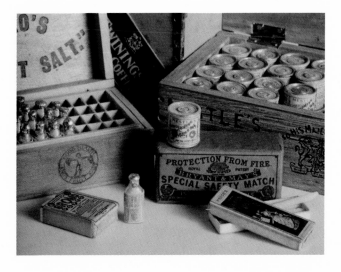

## Inventory of Food Stores

| | |
|---|---|
| 1 chest of Tea | 2 bottles of Salad Oil |
| 2 packets of Tea | 6 bottles of Lime Juice |
| 2 tins of Coffee | 4 dozen boxes of Chocolates |
| 1 dozen tins of Cocoa | 2 cases of Chocolates |
| 4 dozen tins of Condensed Milk | 6 tins of Gums |
| 1 tin of 'Milkal' | 6 tins of Toffee |
| 2 dozen jars of Jam | 6 bottles of 'Bulls' Eyes' |
| 18 jars of Marmalade | 6 bottles of 'Maltex' |
| 1 packet of Jelly Cream | 6 bottles of 'Saltines' |
| 2 bottles of Vinegar | 6 bottles of Barley Sugar |

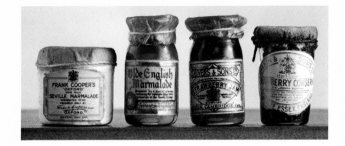

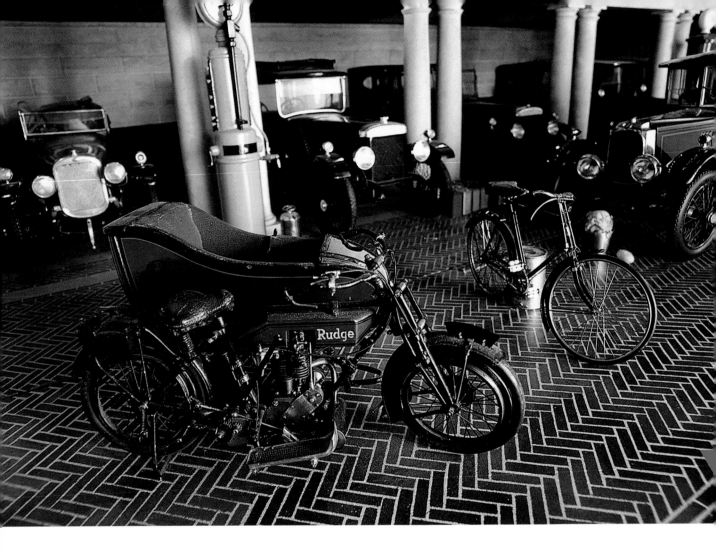

ABOVE: A splendid addition to the Dolls' House Garage is the Rudge motorcycle with its luxurious leather-clad side-car. Also to be found here are the Rudge-Whitworth 'Lady's and Gentleman's Pedal Bicycles'. Lutyens was in charge of the negotiations for these – as he was with Vauxhall Motors – and the firm was concerned that they would not be able to make their models 'absolutely to scale'. 'But,' they wrote, 'the departures will be so slight that they will not fail to be accurate records of the kind of bicycles, etc. in vogue in the year 1922.' *Rudge it, do not trudge it* was the slogan for the firm that started as a bicycle manufacturer in 1868 and went on to produce motorbikes from 1911 to 1946. The Second World War brought its glory days to an end.

# The Garage

Life for the royal chauffeurs in the Dolls' House Garage would have been lived at the cutting edge of motoring design, with cars that gleamingly proclaimed the supremacy of British motor manufacturing in the 1920s. Six of the all-time greats are on parade – all with real engines that would go 20,000 miles to the gallon. They are the Daimler limousine and station wagon, the Lanchester limousine (the firm made the first petrol car in Britain in 1895), the Sunbeam Open Tourer and the five-seater Vauxhall, as well of course as the Rolls-Royce – the 1923 Silver Ghost seven-seater limousine landaulet. During these early days of their production, cars were the prerogative of the very rich, who would have ordered customised models. So it was with the monarch's fleet; in the royal livery colours of black and maroon, each one emblazoned with either the gilded royal cipher or coat of arms.

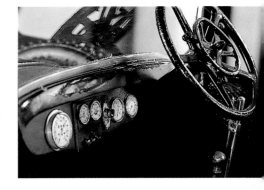

ABOVE: Close-up of one of the steering wheels.

LEFT: The diminutive Rolls, a de luxe version of what was generally acknowledged to be 'The best car in the world', weighs a mere 4lbs, while its full size counterpart weighs 5,200. The most alluring of the lot, this has a silver-topped flask set into its blue brocade upholstery (below).

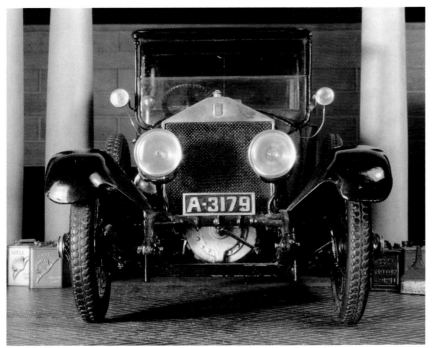

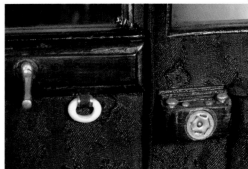

RIGHT: There are two private petrol pumps: Shell and Pratts, the latter the firm that introduced the petrol can to Britain and whose fuel was described as 'The Essence of Refinement'. In 1928 it was to be subsumed by the parent company Esso.

BELOW: A calendar for 1924 hangs on the wall.

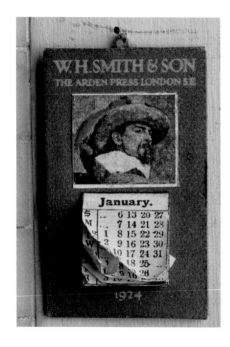

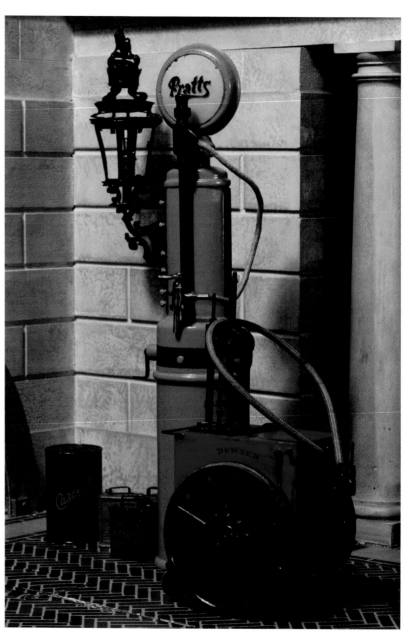

As with stables attached to fine houses, so the Garage for the horseless carriages is here given its full architectural due, with a 'stone' colonnade and rusticated walls, a 'brick' (stencilled) herringbone floor, and a wooden 'inspection pit'. From the all-star line-up, only Vauxhall remains intact, having escaped the various fates of collapse, merger or foreign takeover. Yet here they all are together, as pristine as the day that they were created – in the surroundings, too, that they would have enjoyed in their heyday.

Among the host of ghosts in the Queen's Dolls' House, none evokes more knee-weakening nostalgia than these domestic details; too commonplace in their day to be thought worthy of preservation, yet of such huge and intimate importance to our everyday lives that to see them all again stirs memories of the deepest water.

Harold Nicolson, in his book *The Detail of Biography*, written for the Dolls' House Library, touches on this:

> How rare to the biographer are … gifts of really illuminating detail. Too often does the letter-writer stop short of the essential revelation. Byron himself, most vivid of self-recorders, is guilty at moments of such discrepancies. He tells us of his tooth-powder – he does not tell us of his brush. Or what the Russian oil smelt like, or where he put his paper basket, or spat the tobacco that he chewed. Such are the little gaps and incompletenesses which the biographer of today has to bridge and rectify. And as I contemplate the precision and amplitude of the Queen's Dolls' House, and note how in each detail it reflects the life of an English gentleman of 1923, I am stirred with envy for the biographer of 2023. The works of art, the shaping of the rooms, the furniture, the books even, could be derived from other collections. But with what illumination will he, the future biographer, gaze upon the detailed domestic appliances of 1923!

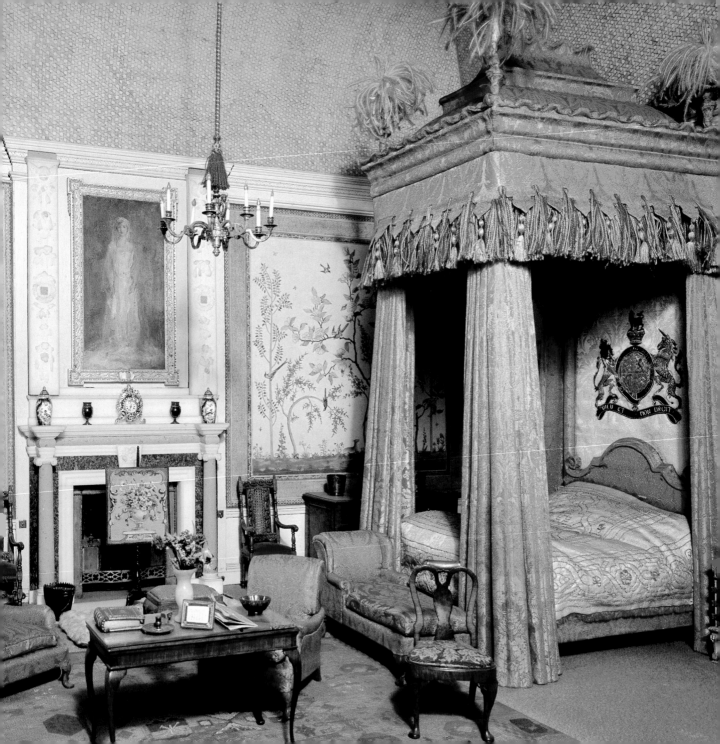

# CHAPTER THREE

# *Above Stairs*

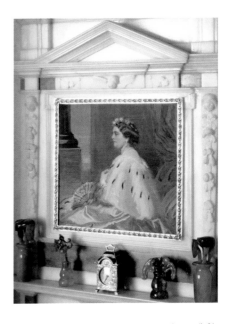

*When, 55 years ago, Sir Edwin Landseer Lutyens was born, the world was enriched by a new wonder: an eternal child, an apostle of beauty, an apostle of thoroughness, a minister of elvish nonsense all in one ... he builds the Queen's Dolls' House, an affair of inches, but such an affair as not even the Japanese cherry-stone carvers could excel ... this minute but splendid abode lacks nothing that a big house would have, and really is such a home as the King and Queen might fittingly inhabit, were some enchanter suddenly to diminish them ... It is as complete and exquisite a model of twentieth century residence as art and craft and devotion could contrive.*

E.V. Lucas
*Everybody's Book of the Queen's Dolls' House*, 1924

OPPOSITE AND ABOVE: While the King's Bedroom (left) is gazed over by his daughter, the Princess Royal, painted by Ambrose McEvoy, the Queen is watched over by her late mother, the Duchess of Teck, painted by Frank O. Salisbury. Salisbury painted twenty-five members of the House of Windsor and, to boot, six American presidents.

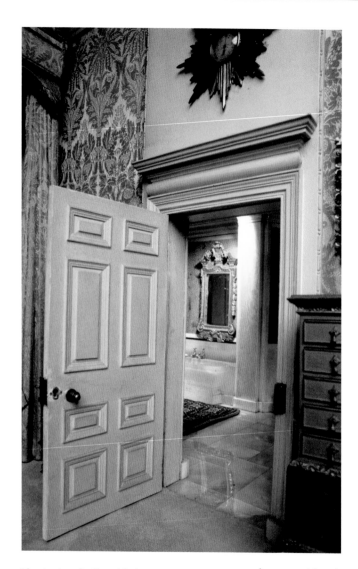

The view into the Queen's Bathroom from the Queen's Bedroom.

Lutyens had delighted in the historic potential of the Dolls' House, enthusing from the start that he would 'devise and design something which for all time will enable future generations to see how a King and Queen of England lived in the twentieth century, and what authors and artists and craftsmen there were during their reign'. In homage to 'Mary, Britain's Domestic Queen' – as she was called in *The Times* in 1923 – he determined that it should be a home rather than a palace, albeit a very grand home, rich with royal allusions. To that end he applied his architectural wizardry, and above all to the royal apartments. Lofty chambers rising two and three storeys through the main and mezzanine floors, the sombre Library and the shimmering Saloon both stretching across the width of the building, these rooms have an exalted yet comforting air. The cosiest and most elevated of all, however, are the royal bedrooms with their brocade-hung 'eighteenth-century' four-posters, sprouting ostrich-feather plumes as they soar skywards to cloud-painted ceilings.

All tiny anthems to the cultivated taste of the times, there are few such decorative survivals as these little rooms in the country. Most large houses built or done up during this period, with a rich mix of the old and new (eighteenth-century chairs drawn invitingly together in the middle of the room rather than placed with stiff formality around the walls, for example), have not been considered serious enough to warrant meticulous preservation; whilst any earlier houses that were redecorated in the 1920s have for the most part been stripped back to their 'original' state by the sterile hand of scholarship.

The Queen's Dolls' House was built so as to preserve an aspect of our nation's history for all time. This was how life was led by the British Royal Family and their fellow grandees, before the First World War ruptured their lives, customs and country for ever. It is with surreal success that time has been arrested within this little building.

As Lutyens lamented that his grand New Delhi schemes were to be the architectural swan-song of the Empire, so he hoped that the Dolls' House would be a 'good tune well sung'. Building for the Queen, he could be in soaring operatic voice, with all the freedom to fulfil his most heartfelt dreams. The miniature scale allowed him to indulge his architectural fantasies without fear of charges of ostentation and extravagance; and in any case, it had been agreed that every object should be donated and that there should be no fundraising on the grand scale. In the event, Lutyens did 'land a fish' or two in the way of generous sponsors. He also, unknown to his wife, loaned £6,300 of his own money, which, according to his daughter Mary, made him 'always rather fearful of death before repayment'.

With pre-War opulence now out of the question in everyday life, in the Dolls' House it could be revived in full measure, although always, Lutyens determined, with the tempering touch of having been designed as the monarch's domestic rather than official residence.

## The Hall

Royal life 'above stairs' was bound, of course, to be rarefied, and would have been surrounded by the work of the most dazzling illuminati of the day. From the moment you step into the Hall, with its white and pink marble walls, shining white marble stairs and silvered balustrade, you are in good company, with the finest output of arts and crafts that the country could produce – company that will keep you entranced in every room. The bronze Venus at the foot of the staircase was sculpted by Francis Derwent Wood, whose work is to be seen throughout the British Isles, while the foremost authority on decorative ironwork, John Starkie Gardner, fashioned the Dolls' House's silver stair balustrade.

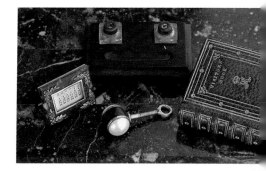

Visitors' book, ink stand and calendar on the hall table.

OVERLEAF: The Entrance Hall. The celestial ceiling panels were painted by Mrs Benjamin Guinness, a British woman who, of all things, founded the Pekingese Club of America. The sculptor of the bronze Venus was Frances Derwent Wood (1871–1926), whose work can still be seen across Britain, from figures on the roof of Kelvingrove Art Gallery in Glasgow, to the great *David* on the Machine Gun Corps Memorial at Hyde Park Corner in London.

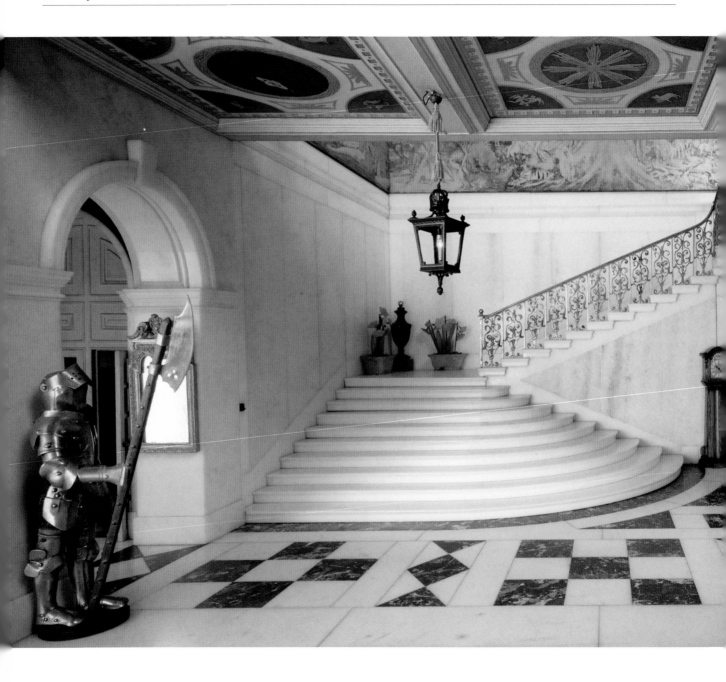

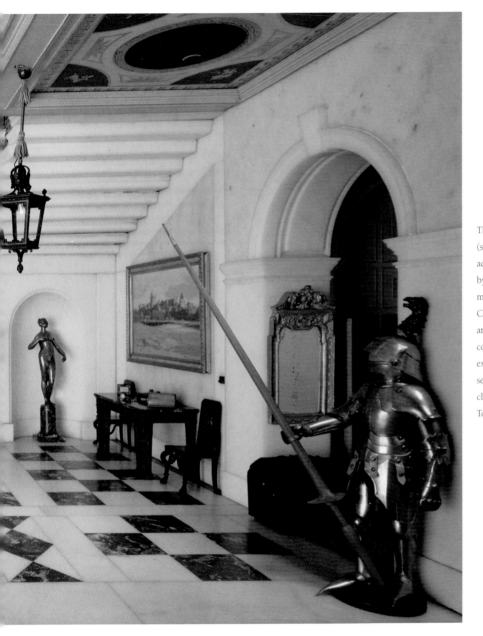

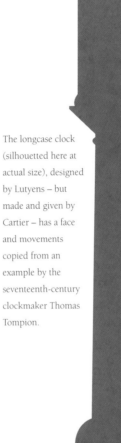

The longcase clock (silhouetted here at actual size), designed by Lutyens – but made and given by Cartier – has a face and movements copied from an example by the seventeenth-century clockmaker Thomas Tompion.

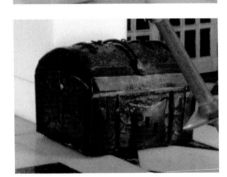

Sweep up the stairs and you can shake the hand of the nation as it were, with King Edward VII and Queen Alexandra, sculpted by Sir William Goscombe John (1860–1952), the Welshman responsible for innumerable figures worldwide, including Sir Arthur Sullivan in St Paul's Cathedral and the Titanic Memorial to the Engine Room Heroes in Liverpool. From niches on high it is the First World War heroes who stare forth: Earl Haig and Earl Beatty, by the official war artist C.S. Jagger (1885–1934), who also sculpted the Royal Artillery Memorial at Hyde Park Corner.

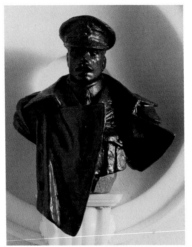

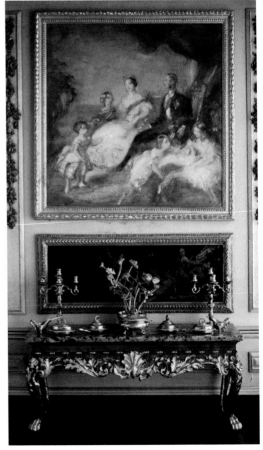

TOP: J. Starkie Gardner (1844–1930) was not only responsible for the Hall's silver balustrade, but also for the great gates of Holyroodhouse. His firm, founded in 1883, still flourishes today, proclaiming the poetry of our age as 'S.G. Systems Products Ltd.'

ABOVE: The wooden trunk, lined with linen and decorated with tooled leather and bands of iron, has recently revealed a hitherto unnoticed handwritten note, claiming to date from 1550.

ABOVE: Jagger's bust of Earl Haig.

RIGHT: Ambrose McEvoy's miniature version of Winterhalter's 1846 painting of Queen Victoria and her family.

# The Dining Room

Despite George V and Queen Mary living, in the Queen's words, a 'Darby and Joan' existence by the 1920s (dining alone together night after night, in stark contrast to the jazzed-up lives of so many of their subjects), the Dolls' House Dining Room was lavishly appointed for entertaining on the grand scale. 'It is a room where parade rather than nourishment is the first consideration' wrote William Newton, the then editor of the *Architectural Review*. Over the doors are paintings by Gerald Moira in

The Dining Room. The list of items for the Dining Room included 48 champagne glasses, 24 oyster forks, 24 finger bowls, 2 pairs of asparagus tongs and 6 slop basins.

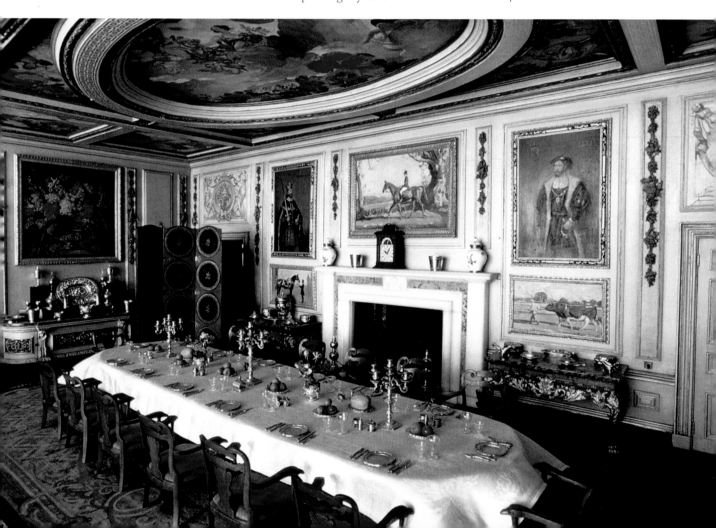

imitation of plasterwork, while carved limewood festoons tumble down the walls in the style of the late seventeenth-century wood carver Grinling Gibbons. Lutyens' carved buffet groans with gold and silver of the 'sixteenth, seventeenth and eighteenth centuries', as too do the 'early eighteenth-century' side tables – 'their legs being exquisitely carved, gilt at the shoulders with lion masks no larger than a sweet pea seed', according to Percy Macquoid (1852–1925), who arranged much of the furniture.

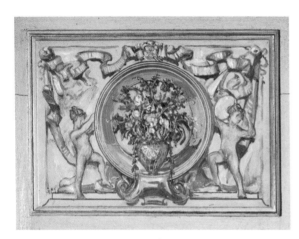

Gerald Moira's imitation plaster overdoors.

Paintings hang densely on the walls, and range from the portrait of Edward III by Sir William Llewellyn (1858–1941), to the more contemporary works of Alfred Munnings, including *The Prince of Wales on Forest Witch*, showing the pink-coated Prince on his chestnut horse, which hangs above the fireplace, while below is a painting of a hefty-looking *Prize Bull*, as well as one of *Delhi*, the King's Charger. Looming large is a copy by Ambrose McEvoy (1878–1927) of Winterhalter's 1846 painting of Queen Victoria with Prince Albert and their children.

A room to feast in, it is also a feast of the decorative arts in itself: the silver wall sconces are miniature copies of originals at Windsor, while standing at the door to hide arrivals from the Kitchen is a red-lacquer screen, designed by Lutyens and made by Cartier out of real eighteenth-century circular Indian *ganjifa* playing cards.

The carpet, which reflects the lines of the richly decorated ceiling panels, was painted, rather than woven, in the Aubusson style by the actor Ernest Thesiger (1879–1961), who was to play the sinister Dr Septimus Pretorious in *The Bride of Frankenstein* (1935). Thesiger was a flamboyant figure whose prime passion was in fact needlework, but who also painted the silk fire screen in the King's Bedroom.

The by-now fading rays of the Empire were discreetly absorbed into the state rooms, to be seen as examples of royal taste rather than the trumpetings of Imperial glory, yet India's presence is keenly felt within these rooms. *The Times of India* lies ready for the King to read in the Library, on the shelves of which you find the enchanting Indian fairy story *The Flute Playing Dolls* by Cornelia Sorabji

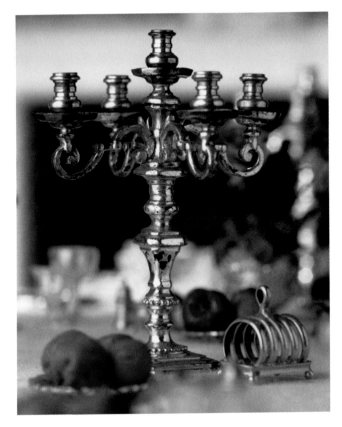

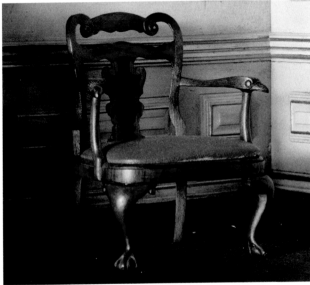

(1866–1954) – academic, lecturer, social reformer and the first female Indian barrister. Richest of all the Indian contributions were the marble and minerals that were given by the Indian Government.

There are also echoes of China in umpteen little objects, such as the tiny jade duck, as well as the Cartier clock designed in the Chinese style by Lutyens. Both these are in the Queen's Bedroom, and both accurately mirror Queen Mary's taste. The secondary staircase, a little extra spine supporting the building, is also in the oriental style. Most obvious of all, in the King's Bedroom, are the painted panels of birds and blooms emulating seventeenth-century Chinese wallpaper, while the many Chinese lacquer cabinets – all the rage in the eighteenth century and again in

ABOVE LEFT: Candelabrum and toast rack.

ABOVE: The 18 walnut chairs, their arms carved with the head of an eagle, were designed in the style of the early 1700s.

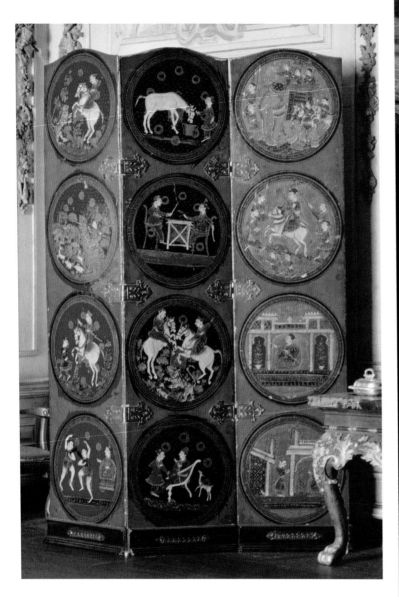

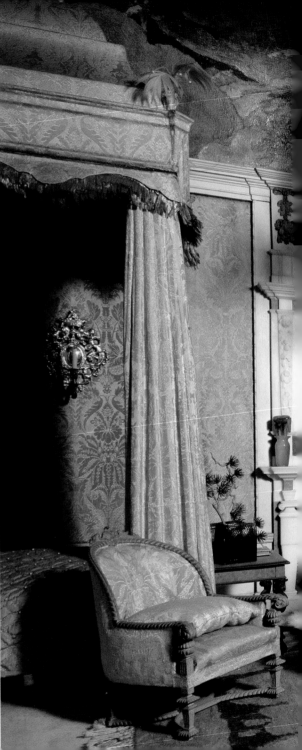

ABOVE: Screen made from *ganjifa* playing cards.

RIGHT: The Queen's Bedroom.

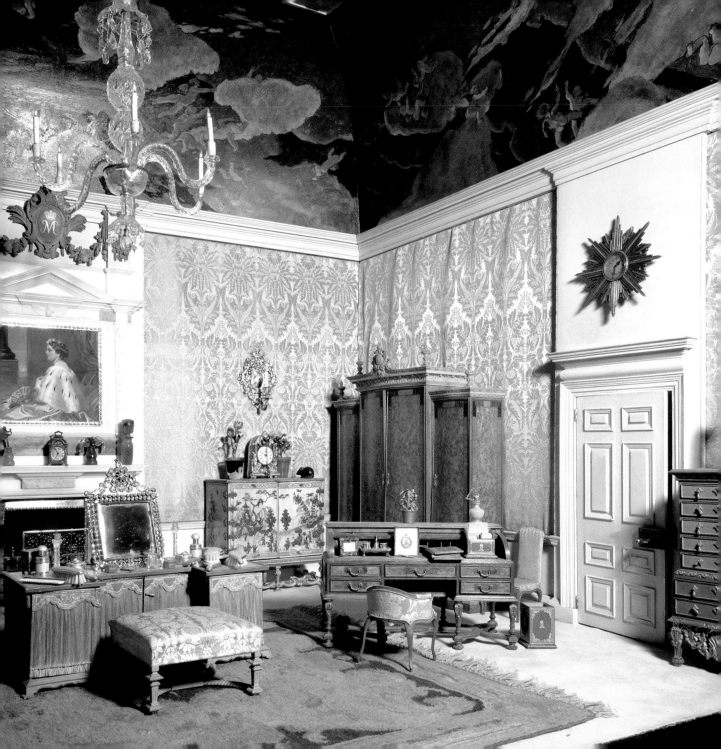

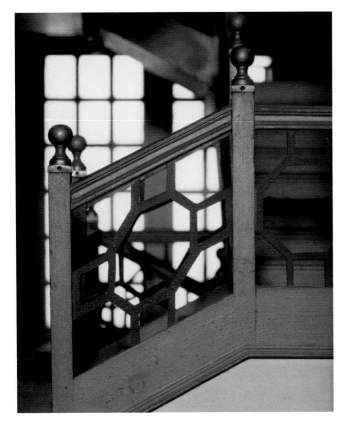

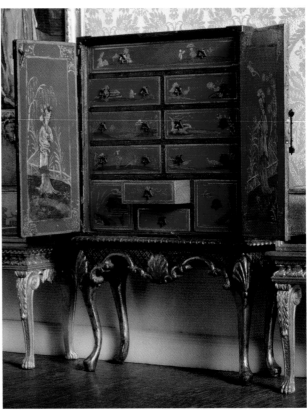

ABOVE: The second staircase.

ABOVE RIGHT: Queen Mary particularly relished the lacquer Londonderry cabinet. She wrote to Princess Marie Louise from aboard HM Yacht Victoria and Albert that her study was too small a room for such a rarity; that 'it wants more space to show off its real beauty'. So it was that this elaborate piece of furniture was given a place of honour in the Saloon.

the twentieth – add considerably to the authenticity of this being a grand house of the 1920s. In the Saloon, a particularly elaborate such example in scarlet, gold and black on gilded legs, was copied exactly from one in Londonderry House, and was given by the Marchioness of Londonderry. What a thrilling subject for sleuthery, discovering how many of these diminutive treasures can be found full-size!

Specific royal references are surprisingly few and far between in the state rooms; although two thumping great silver-gilt thrones, very like those that Lutyens was designing for Delhi (albeit 1 inch high), give the Saloon a most regal air; as do all the gold crowns, set beguilingly atop the gold frames of the royal portraits.

Most overtly monarchic of all, of course, are the Crown Jewels, safely behind the

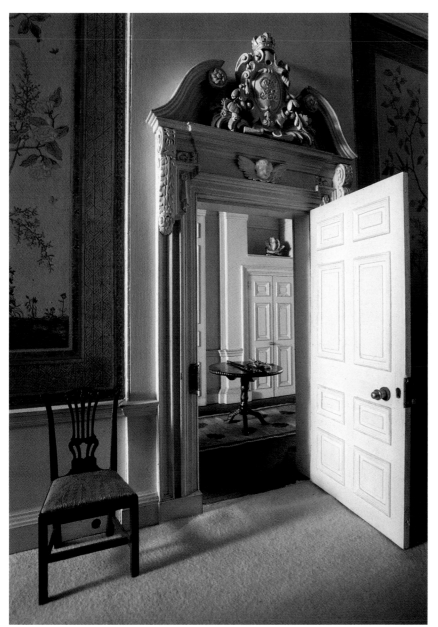

LEFT: Over the door of the King's Bedroom a swan-necked pediment of exceptional finesse, carved with blooms writhed around a royal ciphered cartouche, is topped with a golden crown.

BELOW: Beneath the canopy of the King's 'eighteenth-century' ostrich-plumed state bed the royal coat of arms, embroidered in brilliant colours and golden thread, was worked by the Royal School of Needlework and donated by its founder Princess Christian, mother of Princess Marie Louise.

BOTTOM: Lutyens designed a 'Queen Anne' style bed for Queen Mary, its silken cover quilted with seed pearls. Embroidered over the bedhead a silver and scarlet crown sits above a silver and grey cipher of Gs meeting gracefully to form the letter M.

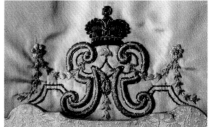

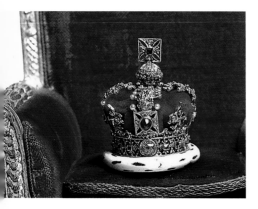

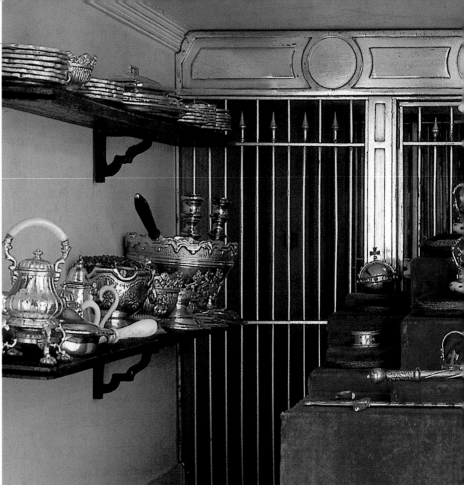

ABOVE: Another gleamingly interesting treasure is the minuscule replica of the Indian Koh-i-nur diamond in the Imperial State Crown, in the Strong Room. Dating from ancient times – some say as early as 3000 BC – the actual Koh-i-Nur was the largest known diamond in the world. By the 1830s it was in Punjab, which in 1849 was proclaimed part of the British Empire. The diamond was subsequently presented to Queen Victoria in 1851. Her daughter-in-law Queen Alexandra was the first to amalgamate it into the Crown Jewels and it was set into Queen Mary's crown between 1911 and 1936, then reset into a new crown for Queen Elizabeth, wife of George VI. Faithfully replicated in the Dolls' House, here the pinhead-sized Koh-i-nur will forever remain at the front of the Imperial State Crown, amid the rest of the splendour in the Strong Room (right).

grill gates of the Strong Room. Weighing 1½ lbs (680g), instead of 1½ tons, the gates are replicas of those with an 'ingenious locking bar' (in full working order) made by the Chatwood Safe Co., founded in 1855. Crowns for the King, Queen and Prince of Wales stand proud – Queen Mary wore her jewels with ample aplomb – and there are two orbs, a sceptre and the sword of state, as well as two pairs of spurs and a pearl necklace. Gold and silver plate for the dining-room table is piled high.

With the two royal coats of arms on the house's exterior, and the sight of Lutyens' crown-topped wrought-iron lanterns in the front Hall, you are on your royal – yet often homely (and always decidedly English) – way.

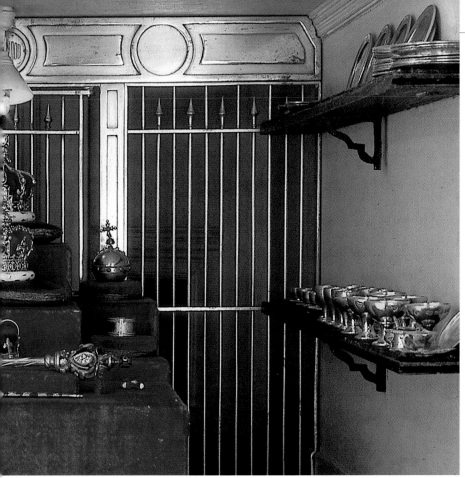

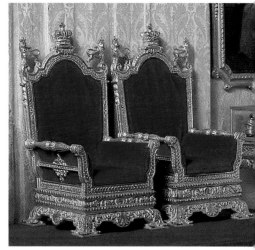

The thrones in the Saloon.

## The Saloon

There are no concessions to ease in the palatial Saloon, with its showpiece suite of eight chairs and two sofas in the stiff style of Louis XV, covered with the finest petit point in imitation of Aubusson. The many millions of stitches on furniture less than 3 inches (8 cm) high were embroidered by a Mrs de Pennington. It is the grand piano though, that is the great delight. Designed by Lutyens, it was made by John Broadwood and Sons and painted by Thomas Matthews Rooke with sensational pre-Raphaelite effect in the manner of Edward Burne-Jones, whose chief assistant

OVERLEAF: The Saloon.

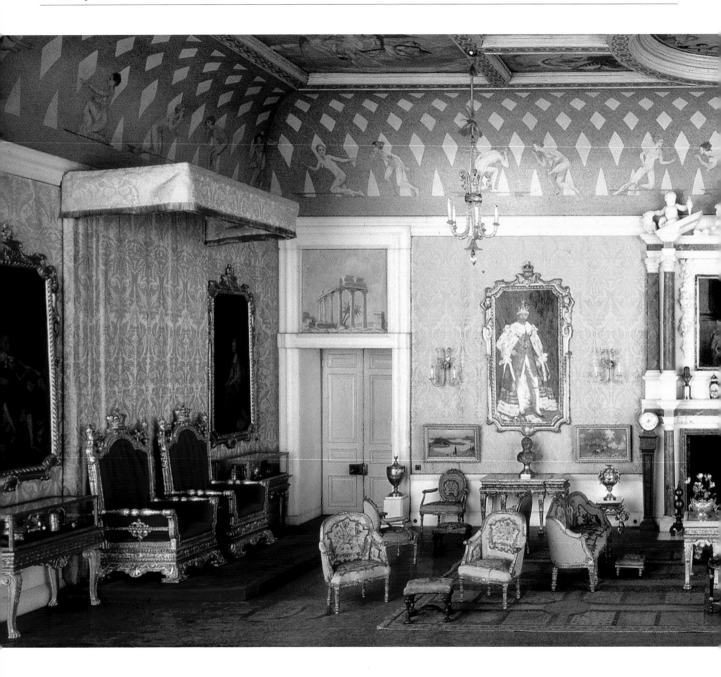

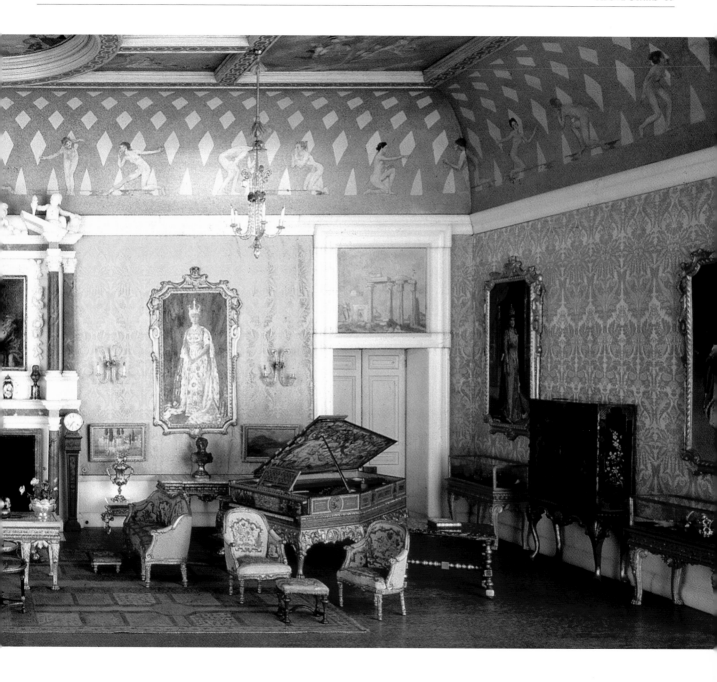

RIGHT: The sofas and chairs of the Saloon are
exquisitely embroidered in miniature stitch.

BELOW RIGHT: The grand piano with painted
decoration by Thomas Matthews Rooke
(1842–1942).

BELOW: The Dolls' House chandeliers were made
by Ninette de Valois' mother, Elizabeth Graydon
Stannus, a glass-maker who, in a great scandal of
the 1920s, was accused of making forgeries of older
glass, despite having written a book on the iniquity
of fakes.

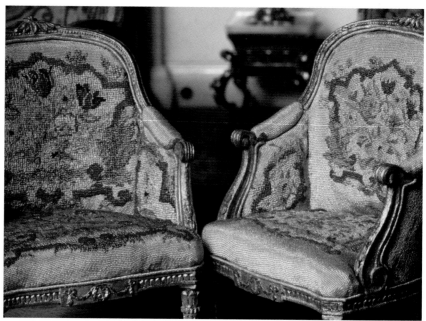

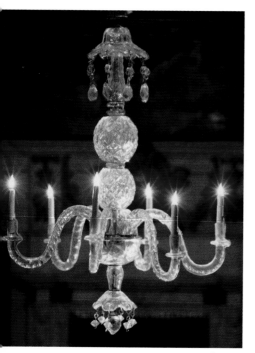

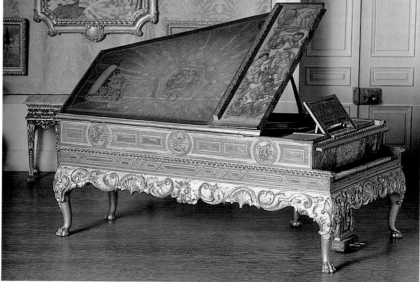

Rooke had been for thirty years. He had already painted a full-size grand piano (now in America) in 1880 in the style of his great master. This must have caught Lutyens' eye; it was at his request, no doubt, that the *G* and *M* were painted over the keyboard. Strange to say, neither this nor the nursery piano, by virtue of their size, ever needs tuning.

Here the crown-topped and gilt-framed portraits of the King and Queen by Sir William Orpen (1878–1931) have such majesty as to defy belief in their not being full-size. The recently knighted Sir William, like so many artists who worked for the Dolls' House, had been appointed an official war artist. So too, on both counts, was Sir John Lavery (1856–1941), whose paintings of King Edward VII and Queen Alexandra also hang in the Saloon. Ruling the roost over the mantelpiece is a portrait by Sir Arthur Stockdale Cope (1857–1940) of Electress Sophia of Hanover, grandmother of George III and the lynchpin between the Houses of Hanover and Windsor.

## The Library

The King's Library too is watched over by royal eyes: Henry VII was (rather surprisingly) painted by Frank Reynolds (1876–1953), the cartoonist and art editor of *Punch* magazine; Henry VIII is again by Sir Arthur Cope (Cope was one of Queen Mary's favourite portraitists); while over the fireplace is Queen Elizabeth I by William Nicholson.

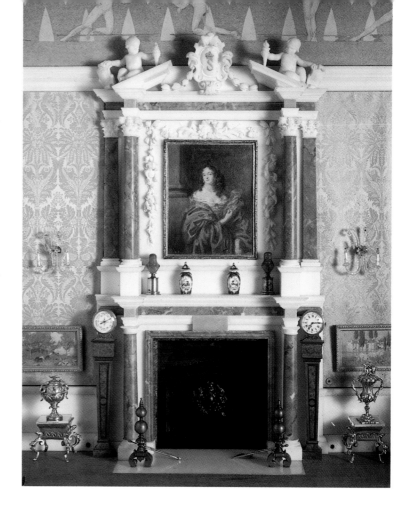

Whichever coloured marble was used to fashion the fireplace, so the room would be designed in harmony about it. Thus while the 'Indian Yellow Marble' in the King's Bedroom gave golden tones to the wall and ceiling paintings, in the Saloon the pink-pillared fireplace and overmantle ensured that the room was hung with rose-coloured damask (pictured above, now faded to gold). Woven in dolls' house dimensions, this has 120 silken threads to an inch, costing the princely sum of £80 – about £5,000 today.

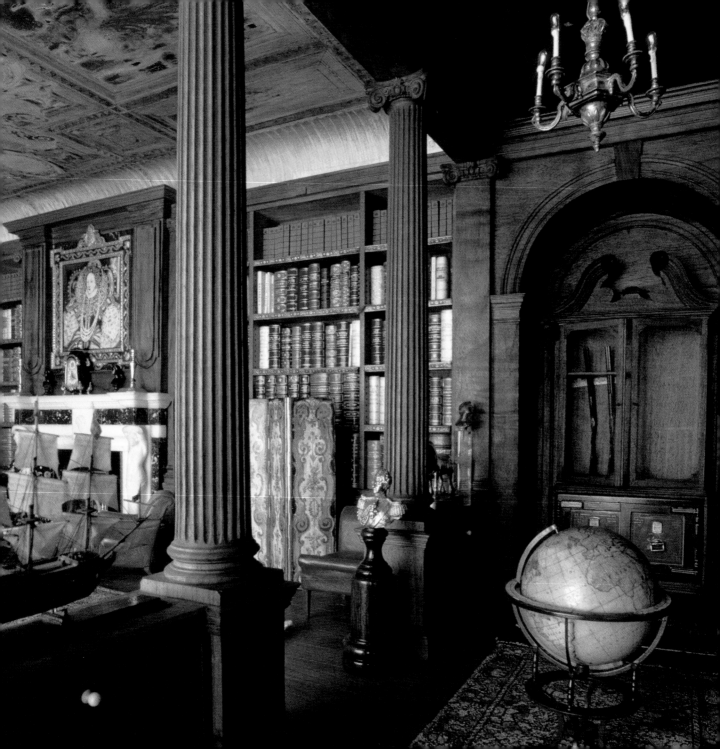

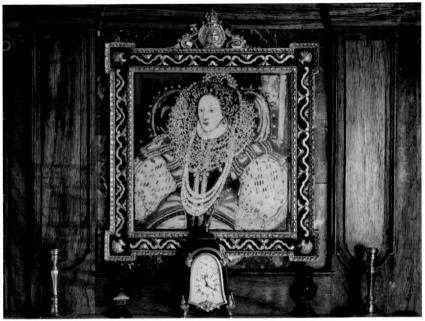

With its handsome walnut pillars and panelling, the Library is a room given
royal gravitas by its assembly of red and green leather dispatch boxes, each
embossed with the royal cipher and 'THE KING'. George V would work late into
the night on his boxes, always in the company of Charlotte, his African grey parrot,
to whom he was devoted. He kept her perched on his finger by the hour and
encouraged her to forage for food on the dining-room table. According to the
actress Nancy Price (1880–1970), when the King was working the parrot 'viewed
state and confidential documents with a critical eye from her favourite perch on
the King's shoulder and sometimes, when feeling that matters demanded active
intervention, she would call out in a strident seafaring voice, "What about it?"'

This room is filled with what was reputed to be a selection of all that was
best in the literature of the country at that moment, and has the type of treasures
that would have been close to the King's heart. (He had never shared Queen Mary's
passion for collecting, other than accumulating snuff boxes.) Here, the bronze

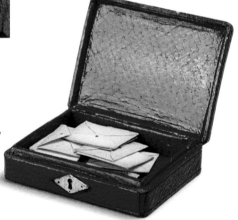

ABOVE: Red leather dispatch box, shown here
at actual size.

OPPOSITE: The Library.

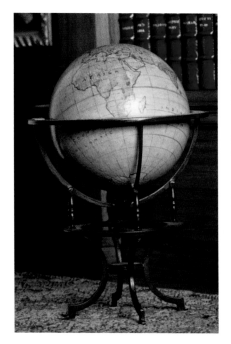

ABOVE: The miniature globe.

BELOW: *The Royal George*.

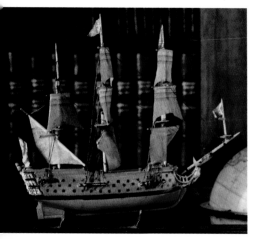

Shire horse was modelled on a real-life counterpart, Field Marshal V, from the Sandringham Stud. This 1 inch (3 cm) high replica was sculpted by the French American Herbert Haseltine (1877–1962), whose giant equine statues can be seen as far afield as Jamnagar in India and the Arlington National Cemetery in the United States.

The choice of ship to be modelled in miniature was a curious one: a re-creation of the *Royal George* of 1788, which met with disaster off Spithead in 1782 while being loaded with stores. She listed over with a loss of 900 lives, including those of Admiral Kempenfelt and many women and children. William Cowper (1731–1800) penned the commemorative poem.

ON THE LOSS OF THE ROYAL GEORGE.
WRITTEN WHEN THE NEWS ARRIVED.

TOLL for the brave!
The brave that are no more;
All sunk beneath the wave,
Fast by their native shore!

Weigh the vessel up,
Once dreaded by our foes!
And mingle with our cup
The tear that England owes.

Her timbers yet are sound,
And she may float again,
Full charged with England's thunder,
And plough the distant main.

The American architectural supremo Frank Lloyd Wright (1867–1959) wrote that he could not think of anyone more capable than Lutyens of 'so characteristically and quietly dramatis[ing] the old English feeling for dignity and comfort in an interior, however or wherever that interior may be in England'. Little matter if the rooms are only inches high, for such is the felicitous feeling in the Dolls' House.

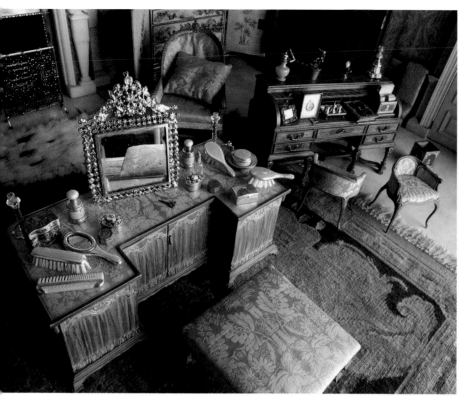

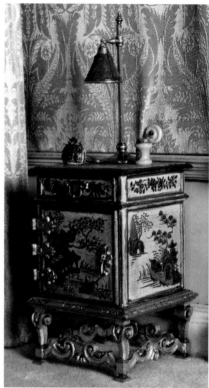

'All is English-made and in the best English taste', reported *The Times* in 1923, while in 1924 Lord Curzon (1859–1925) declared that, if only he had not entered the somewhat depressing profession to which he had dedicated a large portion of his life, he would be a practising architect, building the Queen's Dolls' House for himself to live in. 'Such a house would never be built again', he lamented; 'those who wanted beauty could not afford it, while those who could, desired merely luxury and comfort'.

ABOVE LEFT: On the Queen's dressing table, a mirror framed with real diamonds is surrounded by a dressing-table set of pale blue enamel and silver, including a pot of cold cream; one of the few cosmetics used by respectable women of the period.

ABOVE: The Queen's bedside table.

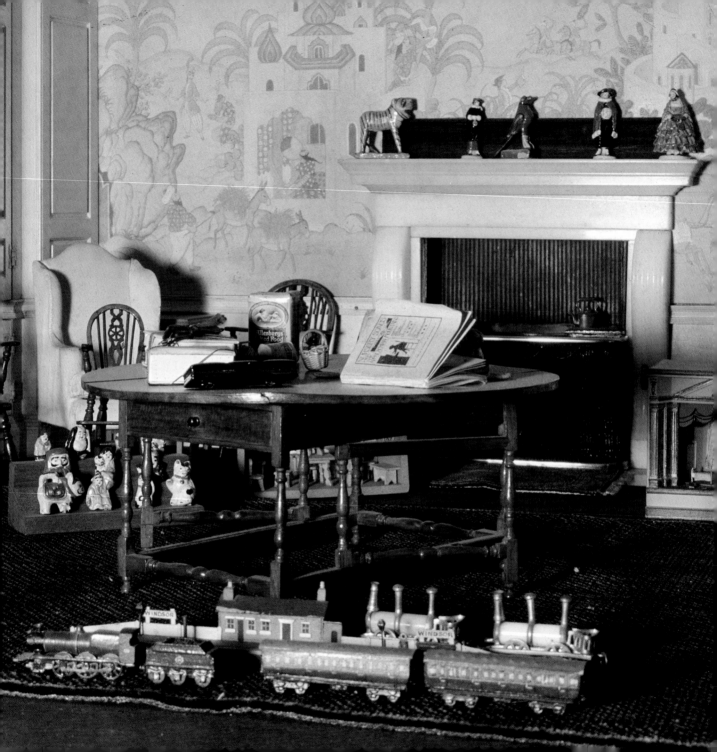

# CHAPTER FOUR

# *Family Life*

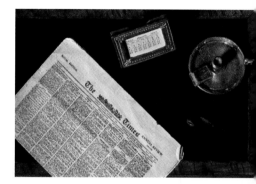

*For the antiquary of 2123 the literary evidence of our current life will be overwhelming in bulk. Staggering amidst the bookstacks in the British Museum … he will be unable to see the wood for the trees. But a visit to the Queen's Dolls' House at Windsor Castle will clarify all his confusions. There, and only there, will be seen the unchanged facts of a life of dignified simplicity in the early part of the twentieth century. Just so and not otherwise could a King and Queen live and move and have their being in a home – for it is essentially a home rather than a palace – made for them by the artists of their day.*

Sir Lawrence Weaver
*The Book of the Queen's Dolls' House*, 1924

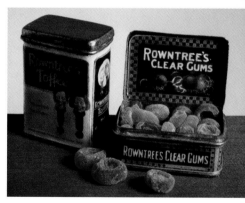

TOP: Miniature copy of *The Times* in the Library.

ABOVE: Rowntree's sweets from the Nursery Lobby.

OPPOSITE: The Nursery, with its toy train, miniature theatre and fantastic murals.

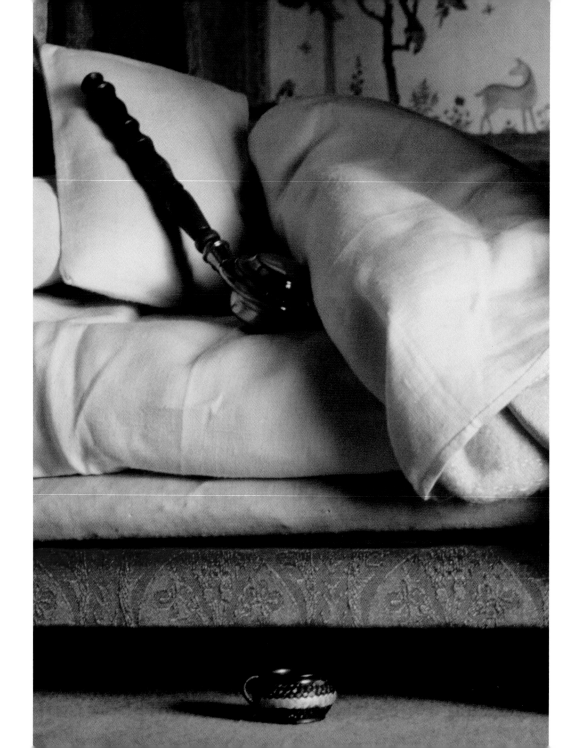

With the Dolls' House on show in the Empire Exhibition, it was suddenly possible for the public to see how family life was led within a royal household. Here were intimate aspects of royal life that few had dreamt of being privy to: how the Queen's bedtime reading was *The English Bijou Almanac*, that she had a well-used silver box of watercolours on hand in her bedroom and that she kept pink 'bedroom shoes' in her wardrobe. It could be observed that the King's bed was warmed by a copper warming pan, and that the chamber pot beneath his bed was painted with an all-seeing blue eye. It was even revealed that his miniature ivory toothbrush had bristles made from hair from inside the ear of a goat, and that the baby Prince of Wales had a bath of solid silver.

The miniature reduced palatial magnificence to a scale that the public could relate to. Whereas in a real palace they would have felt lost and overawed, with the Dolls' House, to their delight, they could feel safely at home.

A dolls' house is by definition a toy appealing to our most fundamental instincts of shelter and the family. As Christopher Hussey (1899–1970) wrote in *Heavenly Mansions*: 'The "little house" is a phrase that goes straight to the heart, whereas the "big house" is reserved for the prison and the public assistance institutions.' So it was that this little building and, most particularly, the family aspects of the royal life it represented, were to capture the nation's heart.

Yet in truth, there has never been a family as such in the Queen's Dolls' House, thanks to the wise decision never to allow a doll through its doors. This was made in 1921 by 'The Committee of the A.B.C.D.E.F.G.H.I.J.K.L.M.N.O.P. of the Queen's Royal Dolls' House ... the Architects, Builders, Carpenters, Drain-inspectors, Electricians, Furniture-makers, Goldsmiths, Haberdashers, Image makers, Joiners, Kipper-curers, Librarians, Muffinmen, Numismatists, Opticians and Plumbers', as the writer E.F. Benson described the company of men and women – scholars, academics, historians, writers and experts – who were in charge of the development of the little house.

One of the most marvellous aspects of the Queen's Dolls' House is that, in its exquisite perfection, the miniature has become magical – as if a real and beautiful house with all its contents, by some wizardry, has been reduced to tiny proportions.

OPPOSITE: Despite the innovatively luxurious bathrooms, both the King and Queen still had a nearer-to-hand chamber pot under their beds (and a warming pan inside). Here, once again, time has stood still: superlative furniture of all eras, set down on wall-to-wall beige carpet: this was how beauty and comfort were enjoyed in the 1920s.

The brass door handles and door locks are now spookily scratched – by whose hands?

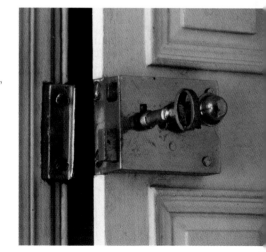

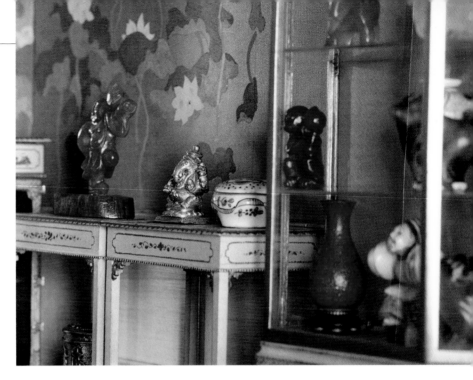

RIGHT: Cabinet of *objets d'art* in the Queen's Boudoir.

BELOW: E.F. Benson (1867–1940), the brother of A.C. Benson, was a novelist and biographer now best-known for his *Mapp and Lucia* series.

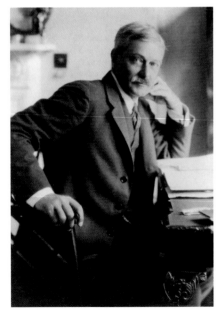

Furthermore, of course, by reversing the spell it could become a real house once again. Hence the banishment of dolls, since one plonked into the midst of this magic would have grotesquely dispelled that enchantment. E.F. Benson's description (in *The Book of the Queen's Dolls' House*) of the Committee's reasoning cannot be bettered:

> A Doll is not a human being in miniature at all, it never produced the slightest illusion of being a real person made magically small, and anyone can easily imagine what a monstrous deformity a Doll would be if it was magically restored to human size … You can look at the pictures, and see what they are meant for, you can read the books, and understand more or less, what they are about … you could … go to bed with great comfort in that bed. But Dolls could have done none of those things: they might have fixed their glassy eyes on the pictures, but they would never have seen them … and if they had ever got into bed at all, they would

probably have been placed there with all their clothes on, because
of their revolting appearance when undressed … Dolls, in fact, in
the Dolls' House would have been the most gross of solecisms.

There are therefore no spirits of former occupants to haunt the Dolls' House,
save for the ghost bequeathed it by Vita Sackville West (1892–1962) in *The Note of
Explanation*, which she wrote for its Library. Instead, the little house is richly peopled
by the spirits of those who created it, along with those of the family for whom it
was created.

So passionately did Lutyens plunge into every stage of the house's progress that
he grew to think of it as his home – as indeed would anyone whose face had been
thrust into these little rooms for some three years. Queen Mary also thought of it as
'My house'; in 1921 Lutyens wrote to his wife that the Queen was 'nervous as to how
the Dolls' House opens … she wants to be able to open it without calling servants!
… Can you see the Queen going hush hush to play?' She and the King once asked to
be alone to play with it for four hours, and Queen Mary often rearranged the furniture.

## The Nursery

Lutyens had given no less thought to the design of the Nursery, adorned with
Edmund Dulac's Chinese wall paintings of European fairy tales, than he had to the
State Dining Room, just as he had taken as much trouble with the Queen's Boudoir
and its jade- and amber-filled glass cabinets – exact copies of those in which Queen
Mary displayed her *objets d'art* – as he did with the grand Saloon.

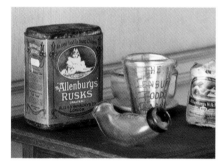

Allenburys' Rusks and feeding bottle, here shown
actual size.

As with a real house, where you can sense the happiness of the home, so it is
that you can feel the Dolls' House's palpably cheery atmosphere, most especially
where family life reigns supreme. Nowhere, of course, is this more apparent than
in the Nursery, chock-a-block with English and Indian toys, with a jar of barley
sugar sticks and a tin of Allenburys' Rusks, with *Father Tuck's Annual* as well as a box
of tin soldiers 'so tiny that a ladybird could push them', according to the official
account of the Nursery by Lady Cynthia Asquith (1887–1960).

Most baffling of all here is what was described in the official book as 'The odd

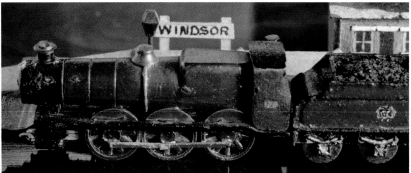

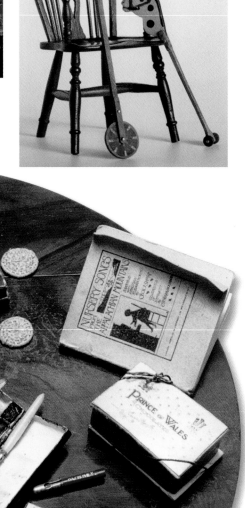

ABOVE AND RIGHT: The tiny Bassett-Lowke steam train – procured by Lutyens through a correspondence with Mr Bassett-Lowke himself, who wrote on his company's exquisite Art Deco notepaper – that draws up at the toy Windsor Station is 10 cm long, the hobby horse only 6.3.

BELOW: Assortment of miniature toys, including soldiers.

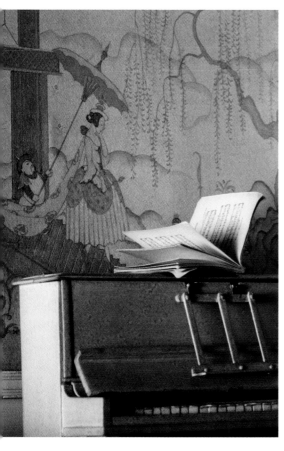

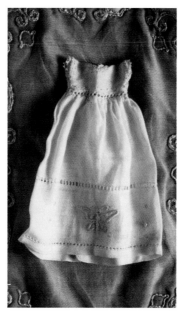

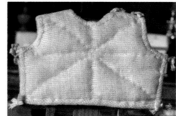

FAR LEFT: *Nursery Songs of the Appalachian Mountains* waits to be played on the upright piano.

LEFT: Child's nightgown.

BELOW LEFT: Pneumonia jacket.

BELOW: In tandem with the times the Nursery has a 'Wireless Cabinet Receiver'. Such models were invented by the British Thomson-Houston Company and only introduced in 1920.

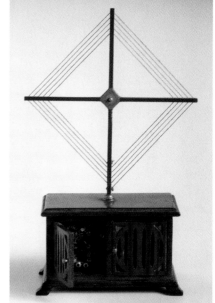

Night-gown demonstrating the Fitting of the Garments'. Most haunting are the children's padded wool-lined gauze pneumonia jackets, worn to keep in the body heat if they were struck by the potentially fatal disease – only four years before Sir Alexander Fleming (1881–1955) would discover the benefits of penicillin.

This little room will be forever embraced by the chinoiserie murals of fairy stories by Edmund Dulac (1882–1953), the French and fantastically exotic star of Britain's Golden Age of illustration, from the 1880s to the 1920s. As with everything that Dulac did, here his imagination has whipped up strange and exciting scenes.

FAR RIGHT: As for the tiny electrically-lit theatre, with *Peter Pan* painted on the safety curtain and two stage sets from the play, this is an enchanting celebration of Lutyens' long friendship with the author James Barrie. In 1904 Lutyens had designed the set of the night nursery for the very first production of *Peter Pan or The Boy Who Wouldn't Grow Up*. He would later tell his children that the story had taken place in their bedroom in Bloomsbury Square, and that Peter Pan himself might appear at any moment to spirit them away. Furthermore, he claimed that it was he who had suggested to Barrie that the Newfoundland dog Nana should be the children's nursemaid.

RIGHT: An elegantly carved wooden cabinet is revealed to contain a wind-up gramophone, made in various stages by some 70 men from the Gramophone Co. Ltd. It is only 5½ inches (14 cm) high and, Dollyleuiah! It works! Complete with records such as *Rule Britannia*, *Home Sweet Home* and *God Save The King*, it was nevertheless banished to the Nursery. Despite Lutyens having decreed that it be designed in a grand walnut case, to enable it to grace any room in the house, it was not to be: Queen Mary wrote to Princess Marie Louise that 'the gramophone should go in the nursery as G. [George] hates them!'

In one a Georgian Cinderella, in an eighteenth-century coach driven by a periwigged coachman, gallops through a cacti-filled desert, whilst on the horizon a wolf in breeches pats Red Riding Hood on the head. Nearby, palm trees surround Bluebeard's domed pink palace, in which the villain sits sharpening a scimitar to kill his latest wife. A frightening green genie, the same size as the would-be children in this Nursery, is being rubbed into being by Aladdin; Sinbad, in a ship with a prow shaped like a peacock, hails Robinson Crusoe and Man Friday, who wave from on high on a steep cacti-sprouting cliff. 'There are magic happenings on these walls', wrote William Newton of the *Architectural Review*.

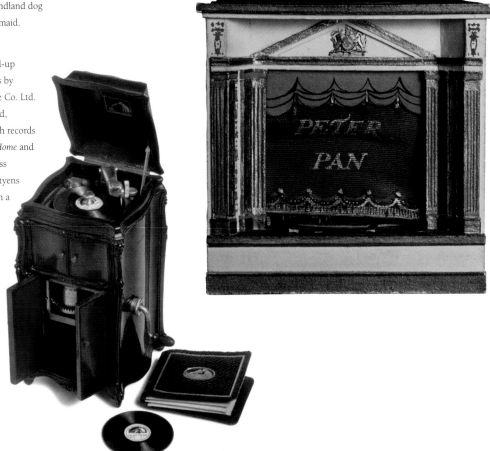

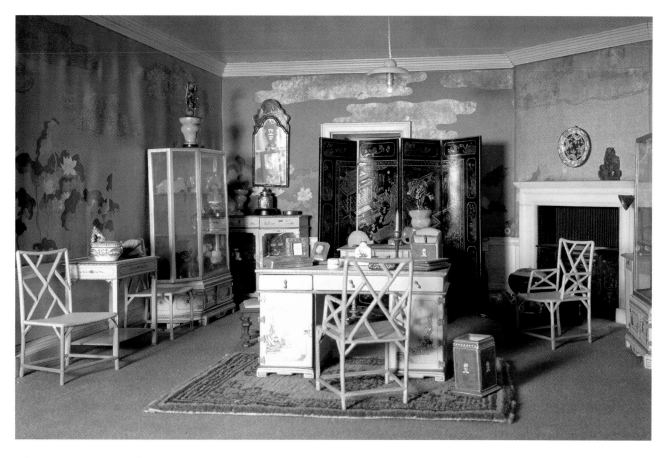

# The Queen's Boudoir

Dulac, one of the most wildly romantic of all fairy tale illustrators, has a popularity that still shows no signs of abating. The Dolls' House Nursery contains his only murals, life-size or otherwise, although he also painted the ochre-coloured silk on the walls of the Queen's miniature Boudoir. Again in the Chinese style, with water lilies and swirling clouds, they are happily in harmony with the oriental furniture of both bamboo and yellow lacquer that was given by Lord Waring, of the furniture manufacturers Waring and Gillow.

The Chinese carpet in the Queen's Boudoir is a tiny copy, with 324 knots to an inch, of a rug of the Chien Lung period (1736–95).

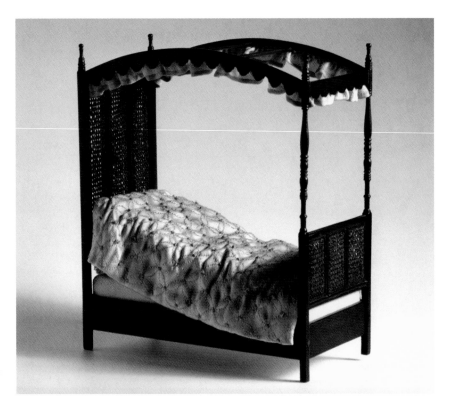

The Princess Royal's Bedroom contains a miniature copy of Lutyens' own bed. In 1944 Lutyens died in his 'St Ursula' bed. 'There is nothing the dead look like except dead', wrote his daughter Mary. 'Father's familiar suits with their bulging pockets hanging in the cupboards had far more of him in them than the empty body in the St Ursula bed.'

## The Princess Royal's Bedroom

Cosily ensconced in family life, the Queen's Boudoir is between the Night Nursery and the Princess Royal's Bedroom, with its mahogany and cane four-poster bed. This is a 7 inch (18cm) high version of one of a pair that Lutyens had designed for his daughters Barbie and Ursula; they are known as the 'St Ursula' beds, having been inspired by the four-poster in Vittore Carpaccio's painting *The Dream of St Ursula* (1495) in the Accademia in Venice. (Lutyens also named his youngest daughter after the painting.) Most suitably for the Princess Royal, when the Dolls' House version was made, a baby pea was put beneath the mattress. Now no more, the pea is one of the House's few casualties, wrought by the ravages of time.

## The Night Nursery

The Night Nursery has what is arguably one of the most entrancing pieces of furniture in the Dolls' House. This is 'the cradle for the Prince of the Blood', as Lutyens called it, made of applewood, ivory and silver. With its hood and body faceted like a 20p piece, all edged and inlaid with silver, it swings between obelisks on ivory-handled spindles. A silver angel kneels towards the baby from atop one obelisk; while on the hood, an ivory cushion bears the weight of a silver crown sprouting ivory Prince of Wales' feathers.

More of a jewel than a piece of furniture, the cradle cost £30 – several thousand pounds today. It was paid for by one of 'the fish' that Luytens succeeded in landing: Mr Frederick A. Koenig, a Silesian banker for whom the architect was designing fantastical temples at Tyringham House in Buckinghamshire.

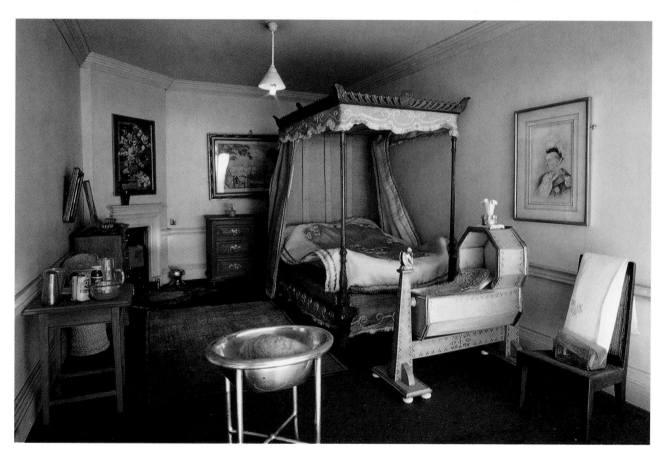

For the baby prince's nanny, who slept with her charge, the grandeur of her mahogany four-poster bed with its elaborately carved cornice proudly proclaimed her place in the hierarchy of the household. The Lutyens family's beloved nanny, Alice Louise Sleath, was with the family for thirty-nine years, every one of which was celebrated with what Lutyens called a 'nannieversary'. When she died, Lutyens designed her headstone with five angels – his five children whom she had helped to raise. This family devotion must have contributed to the splendid furniture with which he honoured the Dolls' House nanny.

## The Bathrooms

The most lustrously shining of all the rooms in the Dolls' House are the two royal bathrooms, with their sleek walls of marble, ivory or snakeskin, all hung with pictures. Their painted ceilings are top-notch beauties, as are their floors of marble and mother-of-pearl. Both baths are curvaceously Lutyenesque; these same forms can be found full-size in houses designed by Lutyens throughout the country. The King's tub was hewn from green African verdite, a richly coloured ornamental stone that is no longer allowed to be exported; the Queen's from translucent alabaster, set down in a room where mother-of-pearl shimmers across the floor and where a white ivory dado and columns set off the green sharkskin walls to perfection. A round of applause please!

In *Everybody's Book of The Queen's Dolls' House*, Percy Macquoid wrote a paean of praise to this room:

> It is one of the prettiest sights in the world to see the bath-tub filled with water, to see the drops swelling slowly from the taps until the whole room is reflected in them, filled with indescribable, minute beauty; and the reflection of the mother-of-pearl and of the paintings on the ceiling, give added colour to the natural iridescence of these globes of water.

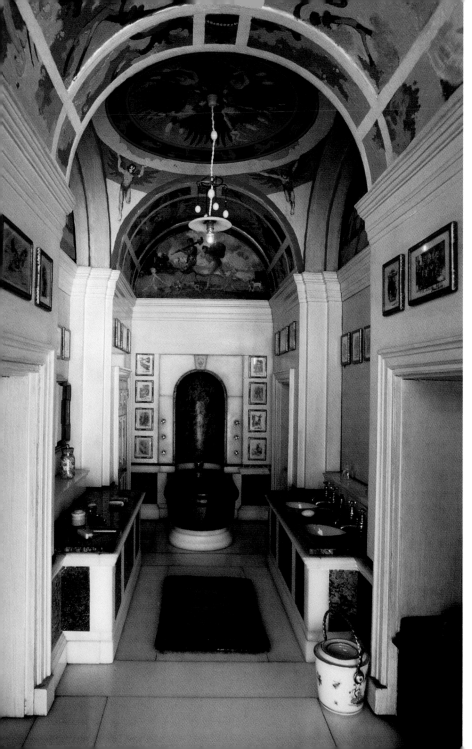

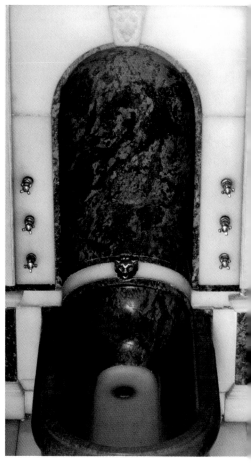

LEFT: The King's Bathroom.

ABOVE: The King's Bath.

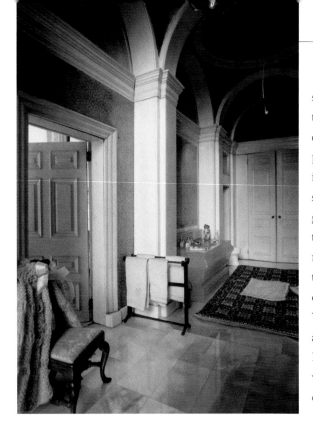

The Queen's Bathroom.

A tiny glimpse into history in these two rooms is found in the sponges donated by Sir Jesse Boot (1850–1931), founder of Boots the Chemist. Almost unseen in an alcove is the Queen's water closet, elegantly disguised as an eighteenth-century wooden armchair and painted gold with cane panels. The King's W.C., more masculine in its plain wooden cabinet, is a 'Valve Closet', with a handle at your side to pull up for the flush. Both water closets were made by the grand old nineteenth-century firm of John Bolding and Sons, one of the heroic band of inventors and engineers as well as producers and manufacturers (not forgetting politicians) who had to fight through the clogged inertia of sanitary reform. In 1963 Bolding was taken over by the most famed of them all, Thomas Crapper and Co.

The mastery of such plumbing in miniature was a marvel to behold and Queen Mary was forever captivated by the cleverness of all the Dolls' House mechanics. Once, when the proud-as-punch engineer was showing her the lifts and the lavatories, she got her earring caught in his beard.

## Games and Sport

Royal and grandee family life more often than not meant a sporting life and in the Dolls' House a games cupboard bulges forth with all the impedimenta of golf, tennis and cricket. The Queen was particularly fond of croquet and a complete set stands by; while for the sportsman-King, two miraculously made 3 inch (10cm) long Purdey guns are ready and able to kill a fly. A cupboard was made for them in the Library, but King George V, renowned as a great shot, was so delighted with their workmanship that he insisted they be laid out to be admired. They are exact replicas of the guns he used and, as with so many treasures in the Dolls' House, you gasp at the dexterity that made them. With what must surely be the smallest double gun barrels in the world, they have smooth wooden stocks and half pistol grips; a top lever and two triggers. Furthermore, believe it or not, they can actually break, load and fire. There is also a little leather cartridge bag, as well as a magazine of a hundred tiny cartridges, the gunpowder for which came from Nobel's Explosives Co. Ltd. The King was also provided with an umbrella and handsome walking sticks, all made by Brigg, 'Royal Umbrella Maker' since 1836, which, now amalgamated with Swaine and Adeney, continues to flourish today.

All the other sporting fronts were also right royally indulged, including archery with targets, bows and arrows, and fencing with two foils, glove and mask. More sedentary games too; most notably with the Library chess set on its tiny 'Chippendale' table (an exact copy of one in the Victoria and Albert Museum) made in eighty-two separate pieces, inlaid with rosewood and ivory squares.

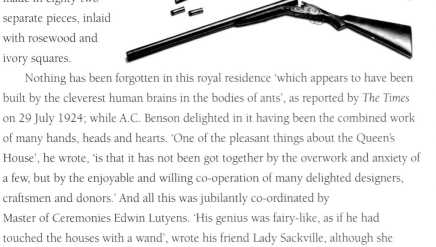

Nothing has been forgotten in this royal residence 'which appears to have been built by the cleverest human brains in the bodies of ants', as reported by *The Times* on 29 July 1924; while A.C. Benson delighted in it having been the combined work of many hands, heads and hearts. 'One of the pleasant things about the Queen's House', he wrote, 'is that it has not been got together by the overwork and anxiety of a few, but by the enjoyable and willing co-operation of many delighted designers, craftsmen and donors.' And all this was jubilantly co-ordinated by Master of Ceremonies Edwin Lutyens. 'His genius was fairy-like, as if he had touched the houses with a wand', wrote his friend Lady Sackville, although she worried that he was embracing work on the Dolls' House almost to the exclusion of all else. That such a distinguished architect should have flung himself so wholeheartedly and with such happy seriousness into this little building – days that he called his 'vivreations', the word he coined for fun – shows the measure of the man.

LEFT: Made by James Purdey and Sons – royal gun-makers since supplying Queen Victoria with two pistols in 1838 – these guns were donated by Athol Purdey, the founder's grandson. They were presented to the Dolls' House in a leather case complete with cleaning rod, tow and oil.

BELOW: As part and parcel of the little arsenal, Purdey presented a shooting stick made of wood, including the seat, which hinges up to become a handle. Called the 'King's Pattern', it was emblazoned with a graceful cipher and crown of brass.

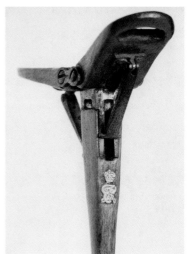

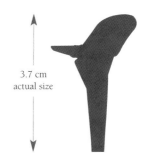

3.7 cm actual size

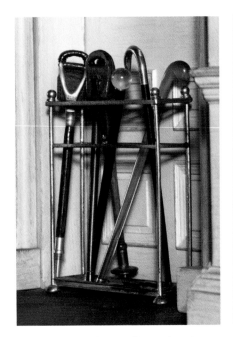

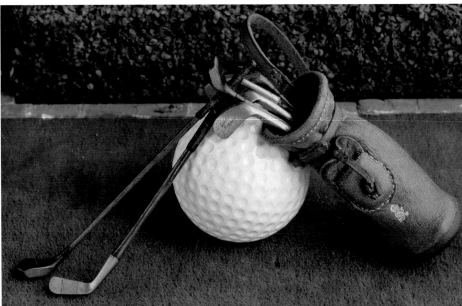

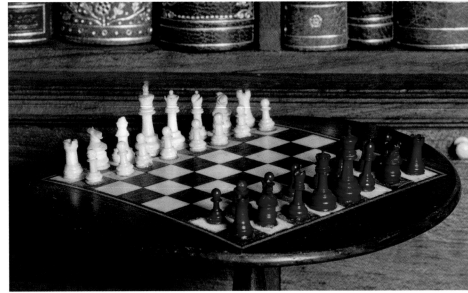

ABOVE: A selection of Brigg walking sticks with the 'King's Pattern'.

RIGHT ABOVE: The Dolls' House golf set laid against a life-size ball. Wooden golf clubs (as well as irons) have their own 6.5 cm long leather bag embossed in gold with the royal cipher. These were supplied by Ben Sayers of North Berwick, who had taught golf to Queen Alexandra, the Prince of Wales and also the Duke of York (before he became King George V).

RIGHT: The chessmen, all made of ivory without a join – the king, at less than half an inch high, is the tallest – are modelled on the Staunton set, named after Harold Staunton, who in 1849 designed the first universally recognised model for chess pieces.

In 1924, the year that the Dolls' House was finished, the youthful architectural historian John Summerson (1904–92) published a sequel to *Gulliver's Travels*. Called *The Queen's Dolls' House: The Palace of their Majesties the King and Queen of Lilliput*, it tells the tale of Gulliver, returning to Lilliput and finding that Lutyens has built a dolls' house as the new Imperial palace for the King and Queen of the Lilliputians. Entranced, the giant Gulliver peers through the windows:

> … upon the rich spectacle within … the Court ladies and gentlemen … with their dainty young, decked out in their finest of silks and satins, and feathers in their hair like an ostrich's but smaller than the down of a sparrow … When I held my breath I could hear Music, played by a company of musicians gathered upon the marble stairs. It was very high-pitched, like the singing of grasshoppers in summer, yet melodious and measured …

So a royal family life has been lived in the Dolls' House after all. Gulliver's only regret was that, owing to his unfortunate size, he was unable to get inside it. So say all of us.

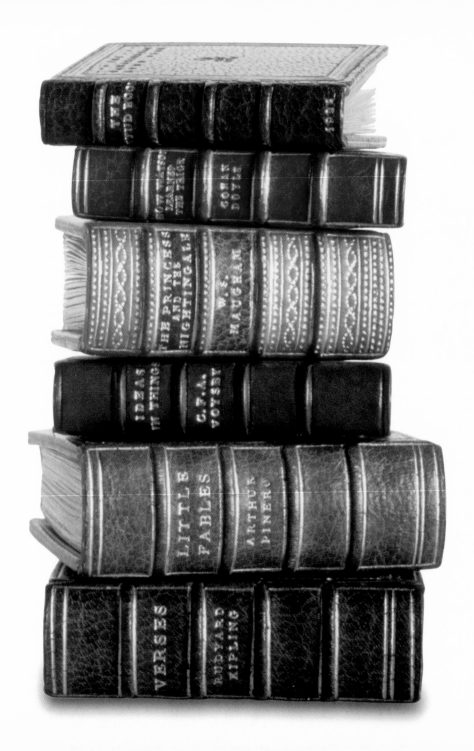

CHAPTER FIVE

# The Library &
# Art Collection

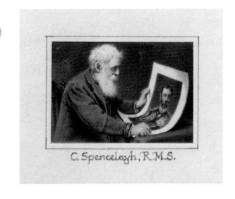

C. Spencelayh, R.M.S.

*How many London residences, even in Berkeley Square and Park Lane, have
a library consisting of two hundred books written in their authors' own hands,
and a collection of over seven hundred watercolours by living artists? I doubt
even if you could find the counterpart of these in the real Buckingham Palace.*

E.V. Lucas

*The Book of the Queen's Dolls' House,* 1924

*... do you not think I ought perhaps to accept drawings from poorer
and humbler people, otherwise they may think the dolls' house is too
"aristocratic" ...*

Queen Mary, in a letter to Princess Marie Louise, 28 October 1922

ABOVE: For *Our King*, Charles Spencelayh
(1865–1958) painted a marvellously detailed face
of an old man, pondering a portrait of George V on
a large canvas in his hands. Gum arabic has been
added to the paint to give the weight and sheen of
oils, which were Spencelayh's favourite medium.
He was a favourite of Queen Mary and this was
his way of painting a portrait of the King.

OPPOSITE: Books from the Dolls' House Library.

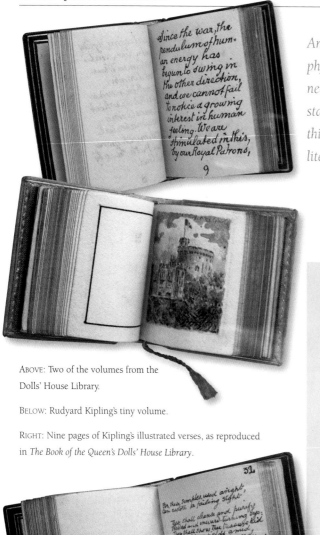

*Anyone who sees the books will appreciate that it was, even physically, quite a difficult task; it is by no means easy to write neatly in a fat little volume about the size of two postage stamps; but it was a labour of love to all, and the outcome of this labour will remain forever a miniature picture of English literature in the nineteen-twenties.*

Stephen Gaselee

*The Book of the Queen's Dolls' House*

ABOVE: Two of the volumes from the Dolls' House Library.

BELOW: Rudyard Kipling's tiny volume.

RIGHT: Nine pages of Kipling's illustrated verses, as reproduced in *The Book of the Queen's Dolls' House Library*.

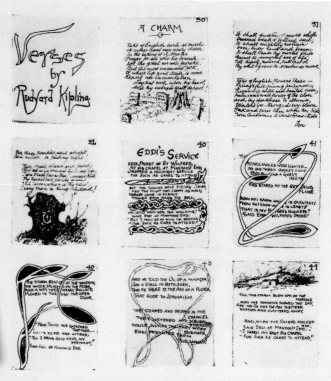

The bindings alone of the hundreds of tiny books in the Dolls' House Library are like jewels – their richly coloured leather glinting with gilded decoration – let alone the incalculable importance of their contents. What value can possibly be given to a 1½ x 1 inch (4 x 3 cm) book of poems by Rudyard Kipling (1865–1936), some unpublished, with over sixty pages handwritten by him in a flowing script, or otherwise in neat-as-pins capital letters? There are also several pages of his unique Lilliputian drawings.

For the poem 'Eddi's Service', the Saxon tale of the priest preaching to a bullock and a donkey as the only members of his congregation, Kipling entwined Celtic forms around his verse; while for 'A Charm' he drew grim trees and gravestones:

> Take of English earth as much
> As either hand can rightly clutch
> In the taking of it breathe
> Prayer for all who lie beneath ...

The Dolls' House Library was to be 'a representative, rather than a complete library', according to Princess Marie Louise, the self-appointed librarian who, with her literary friend E.V. Lucas, was responsible for its organisation. In flamboyant writing – almost as enticing as the honouring request itself – she sent personal pleas to 171 authors and 700 artists, including cartoonists, asking them for donations of watercolours, drawings, sketches, etchings, lino-cuts or engravings. Twenty-five composers were asked for musical scores. To the artists she gave the dimensions of what their pictures should be to fit into the Library's two wooden folio cabinets; to the writers and musicians, she sent tiny blank volumes for them to fill. Once safely returned, they would be bound in leather of every hue, which would then be enriched with an array of tooled and embossed decoration.

Lutyens too was responsible for roping in many of the artists and authors, writing long and detailed requests to such luminaries as Bridges, A.E. Housman and Rose Macaulay. In his letter to the orientalist and linguist Sir Denison Ross (1871–1940), he asked if there were any dolls in the East, and proposed as 'a suggestion ... not as ... a direction ...' that if so, 'might not the English dolls like

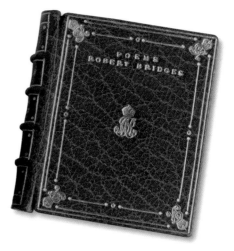

*Poems: Abridged for Dolls and Princes* by Robert Bridges (1844–1930), the Poet Laureate of the day.

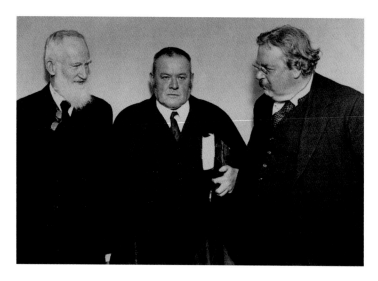

George Bernard Shaw (1856–1950), Hilaire Belloc (1870–1953) and G.K Chesterton (1874–1936) in 1927.

to know about this?' To the critic Desmond MacCarthy (1877–1952) – whose fellow 'Bloomsbury Group' member Virginia Woolf was one of the few writers who refused the Dolls' House commission – he wrote 'I venture to suggest that a little manual on English literature or reading for the dolls would be very acceptable'. In a letter to C.H. Collins Baker (1880–1959), Keeper of the National Gallery, he proposed 'a little manual on the best pictures for dolls', while to the writer Denis Mackail (1892–1971), grandson of Edward Burne-Jones, he hinted that 'something in Latin would be especially attractive'.

George Bernard Shaw was one of the few authors – John Masefield another – who refused to contribute to the Dolls' House Library; '… and I am going to say quite plainly that he wrote in a very rude manner', lamented Princess Marie Louise in her *My Memories of Six Reigns* (1956). 'His letter was not even amusing and, at the risk of offending his many admirers, I say that it was not worthy of one who claimed, as he did, to be a man of genius. I fail to see how he could have missed this great opportunity to have one of his works included in the Dolls' House as a record of an outstanding author in the reign of George V.'

No doubt the idea of his book luxuriating amid the splendours of this royal library – albeit in the company of works by friends such as G.K. Chesterton – would not have been relished by as fiery a socialist polemicist as ever lived. His fame, however, ensured his immortalisation on these shelves: he is satirised in 'Little Fables' by the actor, dramatist and stage director Sir Arthur Pinero (1855–1934), and Shaw's criticism of the poem Chesterton donated to the Dolls' House is gleefully recorded by Chesterton himself. Called 'The Ballad of the Three Horns: an experiment in narrative verse in the metre of the old ballad', it tells of Robin Hood slaying 'The Black Bull of the North / That has trampled spears like grass'. Shaw, with his ardent vegetarian views, was straightway up to his usual tricks, retorting that 'Had the bull not been a decent self-respecting Vegetarian, he could have made a mouthful of Robin Hood'. The poem has fifty-four verses, and it is scarcely believable but Chesterton penned every word of them in his diminutive book. Each verse is four lines long, with one to a page and topped and tailed with a flourish; and Chesterton inscribed them in writing, strange to say, that did not have to be reduced from his everyday tiny hand. How pleasing to think of this immense genius, 6ft 4ins tall and, by 1922, well on his way to weighing twenty-one stone, applying himself to the tiny task. He delayed its delivery 'due to some vague hope', he wrote to Princess Marie Louise, 'of doing something... worthy of so national and historic an object'.

A selection of miniature volumes.

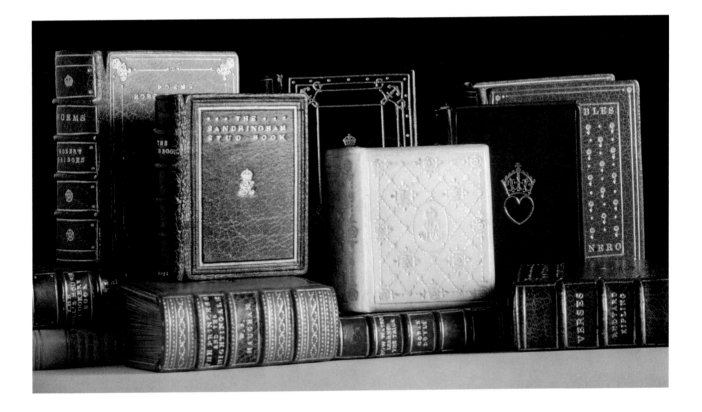

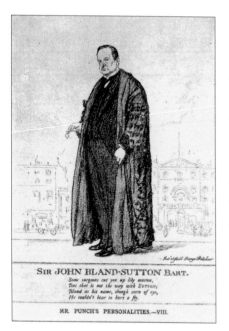

SIR JOHN BLAND-SUTTON BART.

*Some surgeons cut you up like mutton,*
*But that is not the way with Sutton;*
*Bland as his name, though stern of eye,*
*He couldn't bear to hurt a fly.*

MR. PUNCH'S PERSONALITIES.—VIII.

Out on a limb is the *Principles of Dolls' Surgery* by
Sir John Bland-Sutton (1855–1936), pre-eminent
surgeon of his day. Thanking Princess Marie Louise
for the tiny blank notebook she had sent, he wrote
that his little monograph on doll surgery would be a
source of amusement and pleasure. His advice was
far from dainty, with such recommendations as what
to do when a doll's eye is damaged: 'The roof of the
skull is cut off with a sharp knife, as the head of a
doll does not possess a brain ...' and so on, all with
finely wrought diagrams.

The lettered illuminati responded in their eager droves, many of them returning
their completed books within a few days. They were flattered, overwhelmed and
proud. M.R. James (1862–1936) was 'much honoured' and hoped that *The Haunted
Dolls' House* was 'generally suitable' (it most marvellously is). Edmund Gosse
(1849–1928) wrote of his gratification at adding to 'the fairy mansion which will
be of so much lasting interest'; Edith Wharton (1862–1937) sent what she described
as 'doggerel ... unworthy of so charming a destination'. She was right; her poem
'Elves' Library' is appalling. Aldous Huxley (1894–1963) hastily dispatched
unpublished poems by return of post; A.E. Housman (1859–1936) applied himself
with 'delightful readiness', sending poems including verses from his famed *Shropshire
Lad* (1896); while the offering from Compton Mackenzie (1883–1972) struck a
singular note with extracts from *Sinister Street* of 1914, made unique for the Dolls'
House by his putting back all the non-fictional names of the story. Robert Bridges
(1844–1930), the Poet Laureate of the day, then approaching eighty, pleaded that
'neither my hands or eyes are young enough to do such miniature work creditably',
but he eventually sent reams of verses, copied out by both him and Mrs Bridges
'in a more careful script'.

John Buchan (1875–1940), writing that it was a very great pleasure to have
a share in the miniature library, contributed his stirring *Battle of the Somme*:
'... On the Somme fell the very flower of our race, the straightest of limb ... They
have become ... the shining Spires of that City to which we travel.' All these books
were assembled only four years after the end of the First World War and its shadow
was bound to hang heavy over this collection: most moving of the lot is William
J. Locke's (1863–1930) *Miles Ignotus: A Little Tale of the Great War especially written
for the Library of Her Majesty's Model Palace*. Edmund Blunden (1896–1974), the
longest serving of all the War poets – on the front from 1916 to 1918 – sent three
of his works, including 'Behind the Line'. His friend Siegfried Sassoon (1886–1967),
who wrote that Blunden was the poet of the War most lastingly obsessed by it, is
another to haunt these shelves with 'Everyone Sang'. As for Sir Philip Gibbs
(1877–1962), one of the most prolific of all War correspondents; his contribution
of *The Unknown Warrior* stirs you to the very core.

There are conspicuous literary omissions; most particularly the works of T.S. Eliot. *The Waste Land* was published in 1922, the year the library was assembled, but was evidently not thought suitable for royal perusal. (To add insult to injury, the Library has a painting by his father-in-law, Charles Haigh-Wood.)

It is with the Library that you are most disturbed by the lottery of fame, for so many of the authors who were then best-sellers are little known to us today. One of these, Maurice Baring (1874–1945), produced twenty-nine books between 1905 and 1924. For the Dolls' House, he chose to send his 'Elegy on the Death of Juliet's Owl.' Ethel M. Dell (1881–1939) is another such example: 'The most popular English writer of the present day', according to E.V. Lucas, she published forty books between 1912 and 1949. Worshipped by her readers and despised by her critics, she was scorned and burlesqued by both George Orwell and P.G. Wodehouse. Now she is almost entirely forgotten.

There are those, too, who are remembered thanks to a single book: Anthony Hope (1863–1933) has been assured immortality with his *Prisoner of Zenda* (1894) and in the Dolls' House, *A Tragedy In Outline* charts the rise and fall of a romance in a correspondence of ten letters. Again, strange to say, Hope's ordinary writing was exactly the same size as that in this minuscule volume.

From the seventy-one books published by Harry Graham (1874–1936), only *Ruthless Rhymes* (1898) has stood the test of time. Likewise, Hilaire Belloc is chiefly remembered for his *Cautionary Tales for Children* (1907), oddly not submitted for the Library. He sent 'Peter and Paul: A Moral Tale', preceded by an excited acceptance telegram to Princess Marie Louise, 'to avoid delay'. Sir Henry Newbolt (1862–1938) is another who will be forever remembered, thanks to the legendary lines 'Play up! Play up! and play the game!' from his *Vita Lampada* of 1897. Of the poems Newbolt chose for this Library, 'Drake's Drum' is still well-known. 'Vespers' was donated by A.A. Milne (1882–1956), who will be remembered for all time thanks to Winnie the

The bookplates, showing *MR* for Mary Regina, were designed by Ernest Shepard (1879–1976).

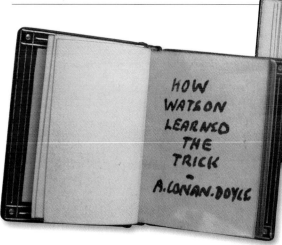

ABOVE LEFT: *How Watson Learned the Trick*
by Sir Arthur Conan Doyle (1859–1930).

ABOVE RIGHT: 'Only a Man'
by Thomas Hardy (1830–1928).

Pooh; whilst Ernest Shepard, the illustrator of *Winnie the Pooh* (1926), designed the bookplates for the Dolls' House Library: these show M R (Mary Regina) entwined above a black silhouette of Windsor Castle with the flag at full mast.

And there are many more stars. Thomas Hardy sent seven poems and Robert Graves sent five. Sir Arthur Conan Doyle created a Sherlock Holmes story, *How Watson Learned the Trick*, especially for the Dolls' House, again in writing barely altered in size from his everyday hand although in a very thick black pen; while Max Beerbohm too wrote specifically for this Library, with the *Meditations of a Refugee*. His hero has always yearned to be very small: 'I approached Mr W.B. Yeats. He looked down at me and said that I seemed quite small enough already…' Eventually, by sheer will-power, he succeeds in becoming tiny. 'When I heard… that Edwin Lutyens had built for the Queen "a one inch scale model of a twentieth-century mansion"… I came straight to Buckingham Palace… I found the mansion. I have been all over it. Lutyens has never done anything better… I shall abide here always.'

Taking the prize for lustrous good fun combined with opulent architectural descriptions is the tale of *The House of The Marquis of Carabas* by the architect Sir Reginald Blomfield (1856–1942). But for yelling-out-loud laughter, no miniature book is funnier than the tongue-in-cheek *More Memories of the Future. Being Memoirs of the Years 1915–1972 by Opal, Lady Porslock*, by Father Ronald Knox (1888–1957). Its narrator is supposedly looking back to 1960s London, and reminiscing about the creation of a gigantic room, ten times larger than life-size.

The Library's greatest tour de force is in fact by a cartoonist, or rather one of *the* cartoonists of the day: 'Fougasse', whose real name was Cyril Kenneth Bird (1887–1965). Popular during the First World War, his influence during World War Two would penetrate into every mind in the land. The propaganda campaign 'Careless Talk Costs Lives' (showing such scenes as Hitler and Goering sitting on the bus behind yakking women) meant his instantly recognisable angular drawings were absorbed into the national imagination. When some years after the First World War, patriotic duty called for a contribution to the Queen's Dolls' House, 'Fougasse' excelled, applying what seems impossible dexterity to sixty-four verses, along with many many more illustrations, telling the story of 'J. Smith'; all written, drawn and painted with a period charm that swirls you back to 1922:

> One night in mid-September,
> While storm-clouds rode the air,
> And a tempest swayed the tree tops
> Stripping the branches bare,
> A fairy was blown out of fairyland,
>     And fell in Eaton Square.

Printed books too play an important part here, as with the heart-quickeningly evocative *Bradshaw's Railway Guide*. There are two Bibles and perhaps, surprisingly, two Korans, while Shakespeare of course has his head held high. With *The Complete Works* in forty volumes, each measuring 2 x 1½ inches (5 cm x 3.8 cm), and bound in red leather with gilt edges, this is the 'Ellen Terry' Bijou Edition.

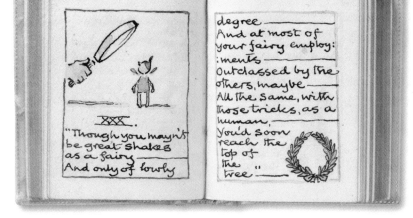

Fougasse's illustrations for 'J. Smith'.

Not to be left out are the four little books of signatures of the most eminent individuals across various fields: *The Stage*, with autographs of the greatest actors and actresses – Ellen Terry's (1847–1928) twirls across one page; then there are the most renowned politicians and officers, who signed their way into the history of

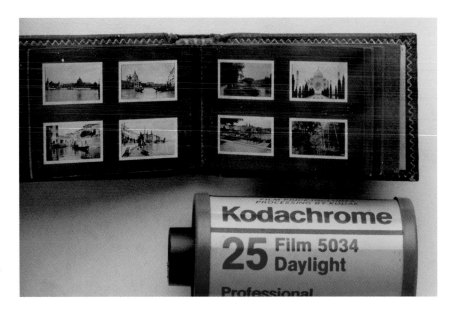

Among the many almanacs and dictionaries there is a tiny album of photographs.

the Dolls' House in its tiny volumes of *The Statesmen*, *The Army* and *The Navy*. Also typical of the miscellaneous masterpieces is *The Sandringham Stud Book*, lauded in its day as having been scrupulously compiled by Major F. Fetherstonhaugh.

The beauty of the bindings is largely thanks to the firm of Sangorski and Sutcliffe. George Sutcliffe was delighted to take on the work, writing to Lutyens in 1922 that 'It will be a pleasurable holiday recreation from our hum-drum work and do not hesitate to send me all you desire to have done though at the same time I would not wish to deprive any of my colleagues of the joy of sharing with me the binding of one of the most wonderful libraries in the world. Mr Kipling's manuscript is really priceless.' C.W. Whitaker was concerned about *Whitaker's Almanac*, lamenting that 'There are certain technical difficulties in the reproduction in miniature of such a voluminous work.' Lutyens was tickled pink by the bargain of the books, writing to the Princess that he had got an estimate for the worth of a single volume. 'A "classic" £600!!!!! Dolly luyah! As we may want 1000 bks, it means an expenditure of £600,000 – too wild for words – but as we must get them for nothing think what the value of the Dollhouse will be!'

With the paintings and drawings as with the books, so many of the artists who would originally have read like a roll-call of honour now appear as a roll-call of the unknown. Who today knows the paintings of John William Schofield? It was with difficulty that I ran one to ground in the Valance House Museum in Dagenham. His little watercolour in the Dolls' House, of a shepherd and sheep, however, makes you gasp at his mastery of light: the last rays of the setting sun, the glow from church windows and door and the moonlight shining silver onto its roof and silhouetting its spire, all of which, remember, are painted in an area measuring 1 x 1½ inches (2.5 by 3.8 cm)!

These pictures are like little stepping stones through British art since the nineteenth century, leading you from full-blown Victorian sentiment (all the artists were of course born Victorians) on to the Pre-Raphaelites and through the twirls of Art Nouveau. The Impressionists are brilliantly represented by the garden painted by Tom Mostyn (1864–1930), with flowers that glow like fairy lights, and marching forth in crispest Modernism – even Surrealism and Vorticism – *Dymchurch Wall* by Paul Nash (1889–1946), inscribed and signed (as is almost every painting) and dated on the back. So it is with the illustrators; all aspects of their craft have been embraced, with such heroes as Henry Justice Ford (1860–1940), who has bewitched generations of children in Andrew Lang's twelve *Fairy Books* (1889–1910) – the 'Red, Blue, Green' etc. Here his *Winged Female* lies next to the work of the band of designers for London Transport. F. Gregory Brown (1887–1941) was one, and his little painting of a house and tree in brilliant hues is instantly recognisable from his posters for London Underground.

In total there are 750 works of art (I maintain that all illustrations fall into that category), watercolours and drawings – in pencil, pen and ink and chalk – etchings, mezzotints, aquatints and engravings, as well as lithographs, a few 'photographic reproductions' and one oil painting (on board) as well as a lone lino-cut. They appear on paper, ivory or even lambskin. Among the portraits on ivory is the all-important Princess Marie Louise; a harmony of yellows, browns, creams and greens painted by Alfred Praga, President of the Society of Miniaturists. Funnily enough, so great was the dexterity of all the artists that the expert miniaturists

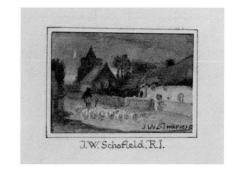

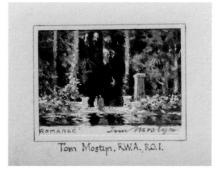

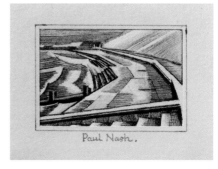

TOP: John William Schofield's watercolour of a shepherd and sheep. These pictures are shown here at actual size.

CENTRE: Tom Mostyn's *Romance*.

BELOW: Paul Nash's *Dymchurch Wall*.

FAR RIGHT: Gregory Brown's landscape.

RIGHT: *Portrait of Princess Marie Louise*, by Alfred Praga (1867–1949).

BELOW LEFT: Dora Webb, *The Prince of Wales*.

BELOW RIGHT: Heywood Hardy's *Girl Riding Side-Saddle*.

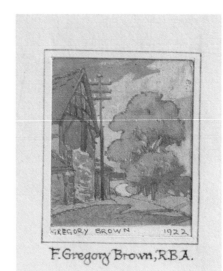

F. Gregory Brown, R.B.A.

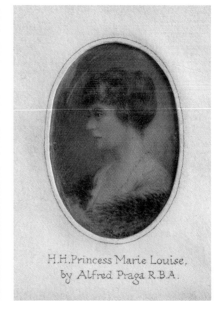

H.H. Princess Marie Louise, by Alfred Praga R.B.A.

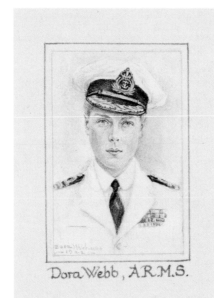

Dora Webb, A.R.M.S.

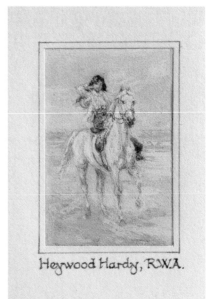

Heywood Hardy, R.W.A.

have by no means stolen a march on the rest. Dora Webb is an exception, having produced a parade of the finest miniatures. They include the baby Ariel on a bat's back; two very-much-of-the-period naked children with golden curls; a festive 'Trilby' (the heroine of George du Maurier's 1894 novel of the same name) with striped pantaloons; and a startlingly moving portrait of the then Prince of Wales, in white naval uniform, with very pink lips and cheeks and with his blue eyes staring forth – fourteen years before the country was plunged into crisis by his abdication.

In gazing upon the many vistas of the countryside and villages, you both marvel and are made miserable in one fell swoop. Whilst the spirits are sent soaring by the artists' quite astonishing ability, they are smote down by the countless glimpses – albeit from an often romanticised and idealised point of view – of an England now long gone. For his *The Approach of Night*, the dashingly moustachioed Glaswegian James Hamilton Mackenzie (1875–1926) painted a man ploughing with two horses on the horizon; whilst Lucy Kemp-Welch, the queen of equine painters, produced the evocative *Home from the Fields*, of a boy riding one of three carthorses. Most ravishing of all is a watercolour of a girl galloping side-saddle by the sea by Heywood Hardy (1843–1933). Horses were painted at the farrier's forge by Frederick Elwell (1870–1958), whose scenes of Beverley life in Yorkshire still have a huge following today. So too does the work of Helen Allingham, the first woman to become a full member of the Royal Watercolour Society. Through her watercolours she set out to immortalise the cottages and gardens of Surrey, before they were either modernised or demolished during the 1880s. As for the picturesqueness of hay stukes marching over the landscapes in so many of these paintings – woe betide the black plastic rolls of today – how many of us remember little private hay stukes in cottage gardens, as recorded by another brilliant watercolourist, Frank Walton (1840–1928)?

Faces too, as well as places, have been preserved for posterity inside these little cabinets. It 'having been whispered' that Queen Mary wanted 'a little picture of herself in the style of the "Old Master"' that Sir Arthur Cope had produced for the House, Cope 'determined to try and do something and, if it turned out a failure …

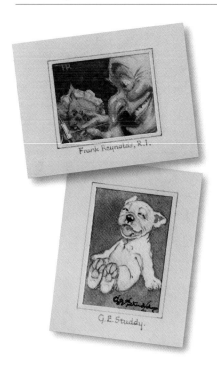

TOP: What, too, of the cartoons, with such extraordinarily wonderful paintings as the huge (relatively speaking) face of Mr Punch with his beady-eyed pug in a ruff, by Frank Reynolds of *Punch* magazine?

ABOVE: Still making you smile is Bonzo the dog, the popular pal from the past created for *The Sketch* by Ernest Studdy in 1921 and named in 1922. Popular enough to appear in the neon lights of Piccadilly Circus, he was translated into six languages, including Czech, as well as appearing in twenty-six films; indeed, the first public film outing for King George V and Queen Mary included Bonzo's *The Sausage Sensation* in the programme. Here he is, still laughing away in their Library.

say nothing about it'. In spite of his injunction to 'say nothing to the Q', to Cope's mock-annoyance the cat was let out of the bag: 'I now gather that that horrid fellow Lutyens has given away my very small secret, and fled to India so that I cannot murder him – yet!' It all ended well, with the Queen writing to Princess Marie Louise that 'George is delighted with my picture by Cope'.

A great loss to the Dolls' House art collection was that nothing came of Charlie Chaplin's proposal – made in 1921 to Lutyens at the Garrick Club, London – to 'give a tiny portrait of himself by himself'. Chaplin actually went to see the Dolls' House being built in Apple Tree Yard and, according to Lutyens, 'was thrilled with Dolly Luyah'. Another absentee is a miniature painted of 'Canada's Loveliest Child', Doris Elizabeth Hyde, whose photograph won the *Toronto Star*'s competition to find 'the child most representative of the loveliness of Canadian childhood'. Triumphing over 7,640 entries (the contest had 'aroused most unusual interest throughout the whole country'), Doris' image was never in fact to grace the Dolls' House: correspondence between the *Star*, the Canadian High Commissioner Mr Larkin, and Lutyens himself suggests that an objection to removing the miniature from its frame of platinum, diamonds and pearls in order to place it in the folios alongside other miniatures – instead of hanging it on a wall and thus 'giving it an importance all its own' (J.E. Atkinson of the *Star*) – may have been the fatal obstacle.

Many paintings by those still considered all-time greats are handsomely represented in the collection; such as the group of anguished children by Dame Laura Knight (1877–1970), giving a great shock as they stare forth. Not only was she the first full female Royal Academician since Mary Moser (1744–1819), but also a dame of the British Empire. Mark Gertler (1891–1939), who in 1916 had savagely symbolised the War with his geometric *The Merry Go Round*, produced a powerful female face in pencil; while the eminent Victorian Sir Frank Dicksee (1853–1928) gave a hauntingly beautiful portrait alive with Pre-Raphaelite influence. George Clausen (1852–1944) has also stood the test of time; for the Dolls' House he painted the watery sun on a bleak winter's morning; for the nation he painted umpteen beautiful – and useful – records of rural life.

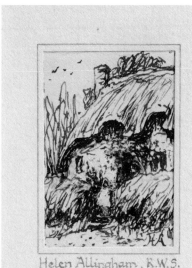

Helen Allingham, R.W.S.

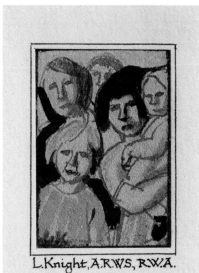

L. Knight, A.R.W.S, R.W.A.

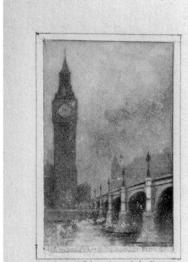

Lucy W. Macdonald, R.M.S.

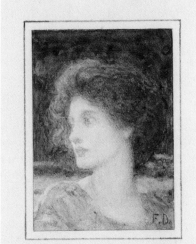

Frank Dicksee, R.A., R.I., H.R.O.I.

FAR LEFT: The contribution of Helen Allingham (1848–1926).

LEFT: Laura Knight's anguished-looking children.

BELOW LEFT: Lucy MacDonald's *Big Ben*, painted in evening tones of red, pink and yellow and looming large over the shining Thames, is an example of one of the paintings on lambskin.

BELOW RIGHT: Frank Dicksee's imaginary portrait.

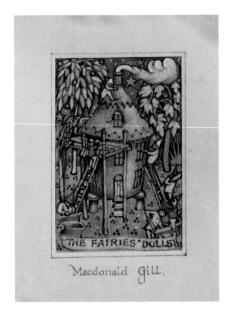

Macdonald Gill's *The Fairy's Dolls' House.*

Two oddities must here be mentioned: Macdonald Gill (1884–1947; younger brother of the artist Eric Gill) presented *The Fairy's Dolls' House* – a scene of strangely elongated red-jacketed and blue cone-hatted fairies, as if Noddy were painted by El Greco, building a thatched house and being watched over by a giant golden bird. Golden stars shine in a bright blue sky. Gill, an architect, muralist, illustrator, typographer and designer, was also responsible for the standard lettering on all World War I gravestones. Another curious addition to the Library is *The Dance of the Three Lotus Lilies* by the South African painter Winifred Brunton (1880–1959), which shows an Egyptian girl against a turquoise background, naked save for three royal blue lotus lilies. Mrs Brunton, wife of a British Egyptologist in Cairo, was famed for her somewhat creative paintings of the 'Great Ones' of Ancient Egypt.

There are so many more artists to delight in. For example, the cartoon *The Growth of Woman* by popular humorist H.M. Bateman (1887–1970) depicts two tiny men in suits, one with a bowler hat and the other a trilby, staring upwards at a skyscraper of a woman, dressed *à la mode* for the 1920s.

The last word though must go to R.R. Tomlinson – a pioneer art educator in his day – with his *Caelo Tentabimus Ire* (the title is from Ovid's *Ars Amatoria* and translates as 'We'll try the sky'). It stops you dead in your tracks. In sweeping brushstrokes, it is an update of the story of Daedalus and Icarus from Ovid's *Metamorphoses*, in which Icarus' wings, made by his father, melted as he flew too near to the sun. Here a naked Icarus, with multi-coloured wings, stands before a pink and blue sky on a cliff by the water's edge, with mauve mountains beyond. Then, suddenly, you spot it: a bi-plane flying on high. What sensational discoveries, one and all.

Of the twenty-five contemporary composers who were invited to send their scores, only Sir Edward Elgar refused, 'in a crescendo climax of rudeness' according to Siegfried Sassoon in his diaries, with Elgar fulminating in rage at the idea:

> We all know that the King and Queen are incapable of appreciating anything artistic; they have never asked for the full score of my Second Symphony to be added to the Library at

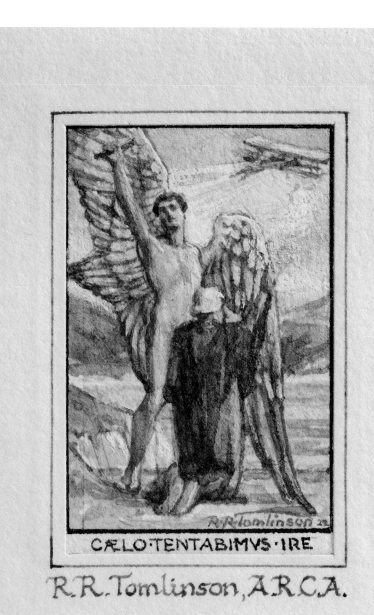

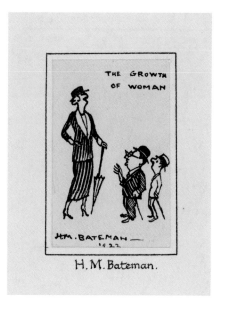

ABOVE: Bateman's *The Growth of Woman*.

LEFT: R.R. Tomlinson's *Caelo Tentabimus Ire*.

Windsor. But as the crown of my career I'm asked to contribute to – a Dolls' House for the Queen! I've been a monkey on a stick for you people long enough. Now I am getting off that stick. I wrote and said I hoped they wouldn't have the impertinence to press the matter any further. I consider it as an insult for an artist to be asked to mix himself up in such nonsense.

Gustav Holst thought otherwise, as did Frederick Delius, Arthur Bliss, John Ireland and Arnold Bax, amongst many more. There are fifty unpublished scores, little over an inch square, bound in leather with the Queen's monogram and all of them signed, with the exception of a posthumous 'Gigue' by Sir Hubert Parry (1848–1918). He, of course, had written the music for *Jerusalem* in 1916. Two women composers also contributed to the Library: the newly knighted Dame Ethel Smyth (1858–1944) was one.

That the work of so many of the forgotten ones – as well of course of the dazzling immortals – may be discovered within these walls is one of the most potent aspects of the Dolls' House.

Miniature music scores by Adela Maddison (1862/3?–1929), organiser of the Dolls' House music library, and Gustav Holst (1874–1934).

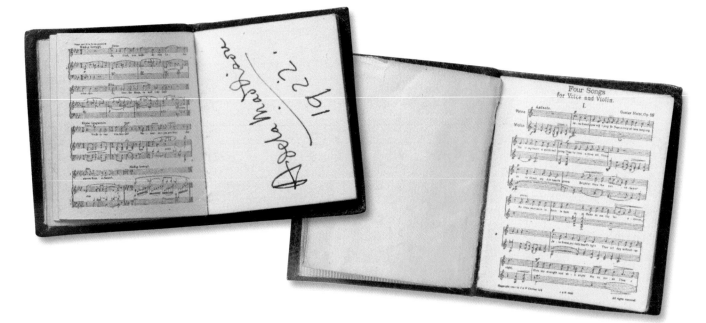

*It has been built to outlast us all, to carry on into the future and different world this pattern of our own. It is a serious attempt to express our age and to show forth in dwarf proportions the limbs of our present world.*

A.C. Benson
*The Book of The Queen's Dolls' House*

What a treasure it is. Never has a generation been so meticulously memorialised: from Bromo lavatory paper to murals by William Nicholson and Edmund Dulac; from pre-penicillin pneumonia vests to handwritten books by Kipling and Conan Doyle. With such sights amidst the wealth of contemporary decoration, art and architecture, literature and music, all enlivened by enchanting contributions from industrialists and manufacturers, the spirit of an age has been forever captured within these little walls. It is nothing short of magical, a word that when describing Queen Mary's Dolls' House can never be used enough.

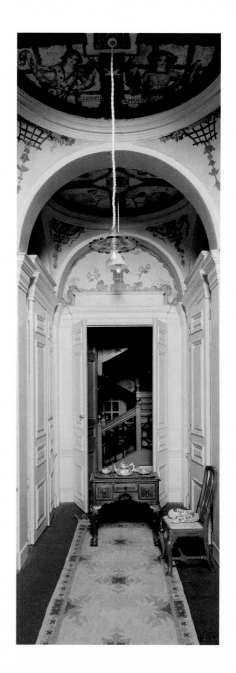

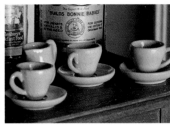

## A List of Makers, as set out in *The Book of The Queen's Dolls' House*

| Category | Object | Name of firm |
|---|---|---|
| Balustrade | | J. Starkie Gardner |
| Barometer | | Cartier, Ltd. |
| Bathroom Accessories | Soap | J. & E. Atkinson, Ltd. |
| Bathroom Accessories | Soap | Lever Bros., Ltd. |
| Bathroom Accessories | Soap | A. & F. Pears, Ltd. |
| Bathroom Accessories | Toilet Requisites | The Diamond Mills Paper Co. |
| Bathroom Accessories | Toilet Requisites | J.C. Eno, Ltd. |
| Bathroom Accessories | Toilet Requisites | Noble & Co. |
| Bathroom Accessories | Toilet Requisites | The Twining Models, Ltd. |
| Bathroom Accessories | Toilet Requisites | Allen & Hanburys, Ltd. |
| Bathroom Accessories | Toilet Requisites | Boots Cash Chemists, Ltd. |
| Beds | | Gill & Reigate, Ltd. |
| Beds | | Lines Brothers, Ltd. |
| Beds | | Muntzer & Son |
| Beds | | P. Waals |
| Beds | | Peyton, Hoyland & Barber, Ltd. |
| Bicycles | | Rotherham and Sons, Ltd. |
| Bicycles | | Rudge-Whitworth, Ltd. |
| Biscuits | Biscuit labels | Jenner and Co. |
| Biscuits | Biscuit tins | Elkington & Co., Ltd. |
| Biscuits | Biscuits | Huntley & Palmers', Ltd. |
| Biscuits | Biscuits | McVitie & Price, Ltd. |
| Bookbinding | Visitors' Book, Blotting Pad | Sangorski & Sutcliffe |
| Bookbinding | | Birdsall & Son |
| Bookbinding | | Hatchards |
| Bookbinding | | Mrs A. Loosely |
| Bookbinding | | Robert Riviere & Son |
| Bookbinding | | The Rotary Binders |
| Bookbinding | | Zaehnsdorf, Ltd. |
| Books and Periodicals, printed | *A.B.C. Railway Guide* | W. Clowes and Sons, Ltd. |
| Books and Periodicals, printed | *Bradshaw's Guide* | Blacklock, Henry & Co., Ltd. |
| Books and Periodicals, printed | *Country Life* | Hudson and Kearns, Ltd. |
| Books and Periodicals, printed | *Daily Mail* | F. Goulding |
| Books and Periodicals, printed | *Father Tuck's Annual* | Raphael Tuck & Sons, Ltd. |
| Books and Periodicals, printed | *Field* | Hudson and Kearns, Ltd. |
| Books and Periodicals, printed | *Morning Post* | Reproduced by John Swain and Son, Ltd. |
| Books and Periodicals, printed | *Pearson's Magazine* | Reproduction by The Century Engraving Co. |
| Books and Periodicals, printed | *Punch* | Bradbury, Agnew & Co., Ltd. |
| Books and Periodicals, printed | *Saturday Review* | Herbert Reiach, Ltd. |
| Books and Periodicals, printed | *The Strand Magazine*, *The Times*, *The Times of India* | The Sun Engraving Co., Ltd. |
| Books and Periodicals, printed | *Truth* | J. Whitaker, & Sons, Ltd. Printed by W. Clowes and Sons, Ltd. |
| Books and Periodicals, printed | *Whitaker's Almanack* | J. Whitaker, & Sons, Ltd. Printed by W. Clowes and Sons, Ltd. |
| Books and Periodicals, printed | *Who's Who* | A. & C. Black, Ltd. |
| Broom | | The Birmingham Royal Institution for the Blind |
| Calendars | | Raphael Tuck & Sons, Ltd., |
| Calendars | | W. H. Smith & Son (The Arden Press) |
| Candles | | Price's Patent Candle Co., Ltd. |
| Carpets and Rugs | | Madame Hayward, |
| Carpets and Rugs | | W. Roberson-Taylor, |
| Carpets and Rugs | | Mrs Rowland Alston, |
| Carpets and Rugs | | The Gainsborough Silk Weaving Co., Ltd. |
| Carpets and Rugs | | Luther Hooper |
| Carpets and Rugs | | Miss Margaret Kinnell |
| Carpets and Rugs | | Muntzer & Son |
| Carpets and Rugs | | Ernest Thesiger |
| Carpets and Rugs | | Weaving School for Crippled Girls |
| Chandeliers | | Crichton Bros. |
| Chandeliers | | Elkington & Co., Ltd. |
| Chandeliers | | Noble & Co. |
| Chandeliers | | Mrs Graydon Stannus |

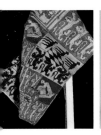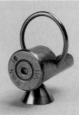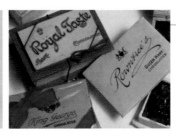

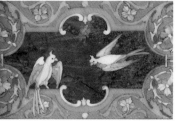
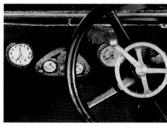

| | | |
|---|---|---|
| Foodstuffs | Nursery Food | Glaxo ( J. Nathan & Co., Ltd.) |
| Foodstuffs | Nursery Sweets and Crackers | J. Pascall, Ltd. |
| Foodstuffs | Swiss Milk | Nestlé and Anglo-Swiss Condensed Milk Co. |
| Foodstuffs | Swiss Milk Tins | Searle and Co., Ltd. |
| Foodstuffs | Tea and Coffee | R. Twining & Co., Ltd: J. Hatfield and Sons, Ltd. |
| Foodstuffs | Tea, Coffee, Cocoa, Jelly, Cream, Chocolates, One Tin "Milkal" | Joseph Lyons & Co., Ltd. |
| Foodstuffs | Vinegar | R. Jackson & Co., Ltd. |
| Foodstuffs | Worcester Sauce | Lea & Perrins |
| Foodstuffs | Worcester Sauce: Bottle | Bagley and Co. |
| Foodstuffs | Worcester Sauce: Red Label | Thomas de la Rue and Co., Ltd. |
| Foodstuffs | Worcester Sauce: White Label | Philips and Probert |
| Furniture | Card Table | The League of Remembrance |
| Furniture | Cradle | Amédée Joubert & Son |
| Furniture | | J. Batson & Sons |
| Furniture | | T. Collins |
| Furniture | | Edwards & Sons |
| Furniture | | Gill & Reigate, Ltd. |
| Furniture | | J. Herrmann |
| Furniture | | Howard & Sons, Ltd. |
| Furniture | | Amédée Joubert & Son |
| Furniture | | R. Langhorn & Field |
| Furniture | | Harris Lebus |
| Furniture | | Lines Brothers, Ltd. |
| Furniture | | P. Metge |
| Furniture | | Nicholls & Janes |
| Furniture | | J. Parnell & Son |
| Furniture | | Barton Prior |
| Furniture | | J. Rowcliffe |
| Furniture | | William H. Saunders |
| Furniture | | Scullard & Bartle |
| Furniture | | R.A. Seraphin, |
| Furniture | | W. Turner Lord & Co. |
| Garage | Vauxhall Clock, Pedometer, Petrol Level Indicator | S. Smith and Sons, Ltd. |
| Garage | Daimler Limousine | The Daimler Co., Ltd. |
| Garage | Daimler Limousine Coachwork | Barker and Co., Ltd. |
| Garage | Daimler Station Bus | The Daimler Co., Ltd., with The Twining Models, Ltd. |
| Garage | Fire Engine | W. Bailey |
| Garage | Lanchester | The Lanchester Motor Co., Ltd. |
| Garage | Lanchester Tyres | Dunlop Rubber Co., Ltd. |
| Garage | Lanchester Wheels | Rudge-Whitworth Wheel Co. |
| Garage | Motorcycle with Side-car | Rudge-Whitworth, Ltd. |
| Garage | Rolls-Royce | Rolls-Royce, Ltd. |
| Garage | Rolls-Royce Chassis, Coachwork, etc. | The Twining Models, Ltd. |
| Garage | Rolls-Royce Paintwork | Hooper and Co., Ltd. |
| Garage | Rolls-Royce Tyres | Dunlop Rubber Co., Ltd. |
| Garage | Sunbeam | Sunbeam Motor Car Co., Ltd. |
| Garage | Vauxhall | Vauxhall Motors, Ltd. |
| Garage | Vauxhall Carburetter | Zenith Carburetter Co., Ltd. |
| Garage | Vauxhall Lighting Set, with Bulbs, Dynamo, Self-Starter and Switchboard | C. A. Vandervell and Co., Ltd. |
| Garage | Vauxhall Magneto | North and Sons, Ltd. |
| Garage | Vauxhall Radiator Badge | W.O. Lewis (Badges), Ltd. |
| Garage | Vauxhall Tyres | Dunlop Rubber Co., Ltd. |
| Garden | Accessories | Abol, Ltd. |
| Garden | Accessories | Thomas Elsley, Ltd. |
| Garden | Accessories | A.W. Gamage, Ltd. |
| Garden | Accessories | H.T. Jenkins & Son, Ltd. |
| Garden | Accessories | Moseley & Co., Ltd. |
| Garden | Accessories | Edwards Patterson |
| Garden | Accessories | C.H. Pugh, Ltd. |
| Garden | Accessories | Mrs G.F. Watts |
| Garden | Accessories | The Whiteside Fitments Co. |

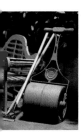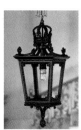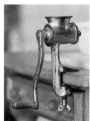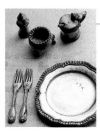

| | | |
|---|---|---|
| Needlework | | Royal School of Needlework |
| Perambulators | | International Baby Carriage Stores |
| Perambulators | | E.T. Morris & Co., Ltd., (The Marmet Baby Carriage Syndicate, Ltd.) with The Twining Models, Ltd. |
| Photography | Camera and Album | Kodak, Ltd. |
| Photography | Photographs | Alexander Corbett, "Country Life" |
| Photography | Photographs | E.O. Hoppé |
| Photography | Photographs | Vincent Brooks Day & Son, Ltd. |
| Picture Frames | Framing | Noble & Co. |
| Picture Frames | | Thomas Elsley, Ltd. |
| Picture Frames | | Amédée Joubert & Son |
| Plans | | Vincent Brooks Day & Son, Ltd. |
| Polish | Boot Polish, Pad, Tin and Brush | Nugget Polish Co., Ltd. |
| Polish | | "Ronuk," Ltd. |
| Polish | | O-Cedar Polish |
| Posters | Paper | Dixon and Roe |
| Posters | Printing | Vincent Brooks Day & Son, Ltd. |
| Sanitary Fittings and Plumbing | Sanitary Fittings and Plumbing | John Bolding & Sons, Ltd. |
| Silverware | Candlesticks (silver) | Miss W.M.Whiteside, A.R.M.S. |
| Silverware | Cutlery | Twining Models, Ltd. |
| Silverware | | E. Barnard & Sons, Ltd. |
| Silverware | | Chester Electro-Plating Co. |
| Silverware | | Frank Finley Clarkson |
| Silverware | | Crichton Bros. |
| Silverware | | F.A. Edwardes |
| Silverware | | Garrard & Co., Ltd. |
| Silverware | | Mappin & Webb, Ltd. |
| Silverware | | Miss W.M. Whiteside, A.R.M.S. |
| Sporting Accessories | Archery | F.H. Ayres, Ltd. |
| Sporting Accessories | Cricket Set, Stumps and Ball | John Wisden & Co., Ltd. |
| Sporting Accessories | Croquet | F.H. Ayres, Ltd. |
| Sporting Accessories | Fencing Foils, Mask and Glove | Amédée Joubert & Son |
| Sporting Accessories | Fishing tackle | Hardy Bros., Ltd. |
| Sporting Accessories | Golf | F.H. Ayres, Ltd. |
| Sporting Accessories | Golf bag (leather) | J.T. Goudie & Co. |
| Sporting Accessories | Golf: Driver and Brassie | C. Gibson, Westward Ho |
| Sporting Accessories | Golf: Putter, Cleek Iron, Benny | Ben Sayers, N. Berwick |
| Sporting Accessories | Gun cartridges | Nobel's Explosive Co., Ltd |
| Sporting Accessories | Guns | James Purdey & Sons |
| Sporting Accessories | Shooting Stick | Brigg & Sons and J. Purdey & Sons |
| Sporting Accessories | Tennis rackets, presses | F.H. Ayres, Ltd. |
| Stationery | Ink | Henry C. Stephens |
| Stationery | Inkstand | Crichton Bros. |
| Stationery | Pencils | George Rowney & Co. |
| Stationery | Pens, Fountain and Quill | Mabie Todd & Co., Ltd. |
| Stationery | Pens, Fountain and Quill, Ivory Paper-knife and Pen-wiper | The Lady Gertrude Crawford |
| Stationery | Stationery Boxes, Waste-paper Baskets, etc. | W. Busson & Son, Ltd. |
| Stationery | Stationery Boxes, Waste-paper Baskets, etc. | Sangorski & Sutcliffe |
| Stationery | | Waterlow & Sons, Ltd. |
| Strong Room | Jewel Safe | Chubb & Son's Lock and Safe Co., Ltd. |
| Strong Room | Safe and Strong Room | The Chatwood Safe Co., Ltd. |
| Structure | Lifting Apparatus | Redpath, Brown & Co., Ltd. |
| Structure | Lifts | Waygood Otis, Ltd. |
| Structure | Steps | Steps & Tables, Ltd. |
| Structure | | J. Rugby Parnell & Son |
| Tobacco, Cigars, Cigarettes, Pipes | | Dexter Bros. |
| Tobacco, Cigars, Cigarettes, Pipes | | A. Dunhill, Ltd. |
| Tobacco, Cigars, Cigarettes, Pipes | | Walters & Co ("Bolivar") |
| Toys | including Dolls, Rifles and Train | Bassett-Lowke, Ltd. |
| Toys | | "Pomona Toys" |

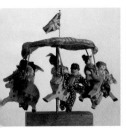
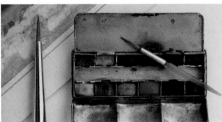

## Catalogue of The Dolls' House Library

| | |
|---|---|
| Delafield, E.M. | *Anti-Climax* |
| De La Mare, Walter | *Three Poems* |
| Dell, Ethel M. | From *The Bars of Iron* |
| Doyle, Sir Arthur Conan | *How Watson Learned the Trick* |
| Drinkwater, John | *Poems* |
| Dudeney, Mrs Henry | *The Feather Bed* |
| Dum-Dum (Major Kendall) | *Dolls' Songs for a Dolls' House* |
| Dunsany, Lord | *Chronicles of Don Rodriguez* |
| Elton, Oliver | Untitled |
| Esher, Lord | *Maxims* |
| Farnol, Jeffery | *The Broad Highway, A Romance of Kent* |
| Fougasse | *J. Smith* |
| Frankau, Gilbert | *Peter Jackson, Cigar Merchant* |
| Fraser, J.G. | *The Reading of the Bible* |
| Galsworthy, John | *Memories* |
| George, W.L. | *History of Woman* |
| Gibbs, Sir Philip | *The Unknown Warrior* |
| Gogarty, Oliver St. John | *Apples of Gold* |
| Gosse, Edmund | *A French Doll's House* |
| Graham, Harry | *Ruthless Rhymes for Heartless Homes* |
| Graham, Stephen | *How the Old Pilgrim Reached Bethlehem* |
| Graham, Winifred | *Royal Lovers* |
| Graves, C.L. | *Norfolk* |
| Graves, Robert | *Poems* |
| Grey of Falloden, Lady | *Star Dust* |
| Haggard, Sir H. Rider | From *A Farmer's Year* |
| Haldane, Viscount | *An Essay on Humanism* |
| Hardy, Thomas | *Poems* |
| Harraden, Beatrice | *Failure and Success* |
| Harrison, Frederic | *John Ruskin* |
| Hay, Ian | *A Very Short Story* |
| Hewitt, Grailey | Illuminated Copy of Kingsley's Poem *The Prettiest Doll* |
| Hewlett, Maurice | *Poems* |
| Hichens, Robert | *The Garden of Allah* |
| Hodgson, Ralph | *Eve and Other Poems* |
| Hope, Anthony | *A Tragedy in Outline* |
| Housman, A.E. | From *A Shropshire Lad* and *Last Poems* |
| Hutchinson, A.S.M. | From *If Winter Comes* |
| Hutchinson, H.G. | *A Manual of Games* |
| Huxley, Aldous L. | Untitled |
| Jacobs, W.W. | *Salthaven* |
| James, M.R. | *The Haunted Dolls' House* |
| Jekyll, Lady | *The Dolls' House Cookery Book* |
| Jekyll, Gertrude | *The Garden* |
| Jesse, F. Tennyson | *My Town* |
| Johnson, Sir H. | *Jeannette Sidebotham* |
| Jones, Henry Arthur | *English Dukes and American Millionaires* |
| Kipling, Rudyard | *Verses* |
| Knoblock, Edward | *The Doll's Dilemma* |
| Knox, R.A. | *More Memories of the Future* |
| Lee, Doris M. | Illuminated copy of Blake's *Songs of Innocence* |
| Locke, W.J. | *Miles Ignotus* |
| Lowndes, Mrs Belloc | *Why They Married and Why They Remained Married* |
| Lucas, E.V. | *The Whole Duty of Dolls* |
| Lucas, St. John | Untitled |
| Lucy, Sir Henry | *Diary of a Journalist* |
| Macauley, Rose | *The Alien* |
| MacGill, Patrick | *Wee Red-Headed Man* |
| Mackenzie, Compton | *Richard Gunstone* from *Sinister Street* |
| Mallock, W.H. | *Verses* and an Extract from *The New Little Things* |
| Marriott, Charles | *Little Things* |
| Marsh, Edward | Georgian Poetry, chosen and copied out by |
| Marshall, Archibald | *The Twins and Miss Bird* from *The Eldest Son* |
| Mason, A.E.W. | *The Silver Ship* |
| Maugham, William Somerset | *The Princess and the Nightingale* |
| Maxwell, W.B. | *The Companions* |
| McKenna, Stephen | *Sonia, Between Two Worlds, A Novel* |
| Merrick, Leonard | *Conrad in Quest of His Youth* |
| Meynell, Alice | *Poems* |
| Milne, A.A. | *Vespers* |
| Moore, F. Frankfort | *The Way to Keep Him* |
| Mordaunt, Elinor | *The Garden of Contentment* |
| Morgan, Evan | *Poems* |
| Newbolt, Sir Henry | *Poems* |
| Nicolson, The Hon. Harold | *The Detail of Biography* |
| Norris, W.E. | *A Peasant of Lorraine* |
| Noyes, Alfred | *The Elfin Artist* |
| Ole-Luk-Oie (Major-Gen. Ernest Dunlop Swinton, C.B.) | *What the Mulberry Saw* |
| Oppenheim, E. Phillips | *The Villa Deveron* |
| Pain, Barry | *Maud* |
| Pemberton, Max | *Lion Heart* |
| Pennell, J. | *Thoughts* |
| Phillpotts, Eden | *The River Dart* |
| Pinero, Sir A.W. | *Little Fables* |
| Pollock, Sir Frederick | *Queen Titania's Chancellor* |
| Quiller-Couch, Sir Arthur | *Verses* |
| Ridge, William Pett | *Mord Em'ly* |
| Rita (Mrs W.D. Humphreys) | *The Road to Anywhere* |
| Robins, Elizabeth | *Come and Find Me* |

## List of Composers

## Artists who contributed to the portraits, paintings, wall and ceiling decoration and other ornamentation

Philpot, Glyn
Pinks, R.A.
Plank, George
Pryse, Captain Spenser
Ramsay, The Lady Patricia
Ranken, W.B.E.
Reynolds, Frank
Raven-Hill, L.
Rispin, Rowland
Rooke, T.M.
Sacco, George
Salisbury, F.O.
Sclanders, Miss
Shepard, E.H.
Silas, Louis
Sims, Charles
Stokes, Adrian
Thomas, Cecil
Van Anrooy, A.
Walcot, W.
Wood, Prof. F. Derwent

## Artists whose work is stored in the Special Cabinets of the Library

Adams, Chris
Adams, H.W.
Adams, P.W.
Adams, W. Dacres
Airy, Anna
Aldin, Cecil
Alexander, Herbert
Allen, W.H.
Allingham, Helen
Alsop, J.J.
Alsop, Mrs
Anderson, Stanley
Armington, Caroline
Armington, Frank M.
Armstrong, C.
Austen, Winifred
Badeley, J.
Badham, E.L.

Baird, N.H.J.
Baker, Miss B.
Baker, Oliver
Baker, S.
Baness, Mrs Mary
Bardill, Ralph W.
Barraclough, J.P.
Barton, Rose
Baskett, C.H.
Bateman, H.M.
Baumer, Lewis
Bayes, Jessie
Beaumont, Prof. Ivor
Bebb, Rosa
Bedford, Francis D.
Belcher, George
Bell, Mrs G.K.M.
Benger, Berenger
Bennett, Florence E.
Bentley, Alfred
Berie, John A.
Birch, S.J. Lamorna
Birley, Oswald H.
Bishop, W.F.
Black, Miss A.S.
Black, Arthur J.
Black, F.
Blampied, Clifford G.
Board, Ernest
Booth, S. Lawson
Borthwick, A.E.
Bottomley, A.E.
Bottomley, Edwin
Bourne, Miss N.B.
Bowen, Owen
Bradshaw, Constance H.
Brewer, Henry C.
Brinson, J. Paul
Broadhead, Miss M.E.
Brock, C.E.
Brock, H.M.
Brockbank, Elizabeth
Brockhurst, G.L.
Brooks, Mrs Maie L.
Brown, Arnesby, R.A.
Brown, F. Gregory

Brown, T. Austen
Browne, G. Washington
Browne, Gordon
Browning, Miss A.K.
Bruhl, L. Burleigh
Brunton, Mrs W.
Bryant, Charles
Bryce, A.J.C.
Buchanan, Inez
Buchel, C.A.
Bulleid, G. Lawrence
Burgess, Arthur J.
Burgess, Miss E.M.
Burke, Harold
Burleigh, C.H.H.
Burne-Jones, Sir Philip
Burnett, C. Ross
Burridge, F.V.
Burrington, Arthur
Bush, R.E.J.
Butler, Lady E.
Butler, Mildred A.
Cafe, T. Watt
Callcott, Mrs F.T. (Florence Newman)
Cameron, D.Y.
Cameron, Katharine
Carter, Frank W.
Chappel, E.
Charlton, E.W.
Charlton, George
Chilton, Margaret
Clark, Christopher
Clark, James Cosmos
Clarke, Miss E. Thornton
Clausen, George
Clifford, H. Charles
Clough, Tom
Clutterbuck, J.E.
Coates, G.J.
Coates, Mrs G.
Cockram, George
Cole, Herbert
Cole, Rex Vicat
Collier, The Hon. John
Collins, A.H.
Collins, G.E.

Collins, W.W.
Comley, J.W.
Conder, Helen E.
Connaught, H.R.H. Princess Patricia of, see Ramsay, Lady Patricia
Cooper, A.E.
Cope, Sir A.S.
Copeman, Miss C.G.
Court, Emily
Cowper, F. Cadogan
Cox, E.A.
Cox, Miss O.S.
Crockett, H.E.
Cursiter, Capt. Stanley
Dadd, Frank
Da Fano, Mrs Dorothea Landau
Davidson, Allan A.
Dawson, Nelson
Day, W. Cave
De Glehn, W.G.
Dening, C.F.W.
Dennis, Ada
Detmold, Edward J.
De Walton, John
Dexter, Walter
Dicksee, Frank
Dicksee, Herbert
Dixon, Charles
Dixon, Percy
Dobson, H.J.
Dollman, J.C.
Douglas, Hope
Dow, A. Warren
Downie, Patrick
Downs, Edgar
Drew, Herbert J.
Drinkwater, George C.
Duff, J.R.K.
Dugdale, T.C.
Eadie, Kate M.
Eadie, Robert
Eden, Denis
Edmunds, Nellie M. Hepburn
Eggington, W.
Ehler, E.H.
Elgood, George S.

'O! I saw one of your gentlemen footmen today outside your Highness's Palace!' Lutyens was fond of illustrating his letters to the Princess, as this little doodle in a letter of 1921 shows. With his tiny twists of merriment – ending one of his letters to Princess Marie Louise with 'Yours obediently and diminutively' – Lutyens relished every aspect of working on the Dolls' House. But it was not only Lutyens whose sense of fun was brought to the fore by work on the miniature House; the 'only anxiety' for the artist Walter Bayes was 'lest after so much talent had been expended in producing toy architecture, toy pictures and toy furniture, an envious Bolshevik might introduce a toy bomb and – and that would be a pity.'

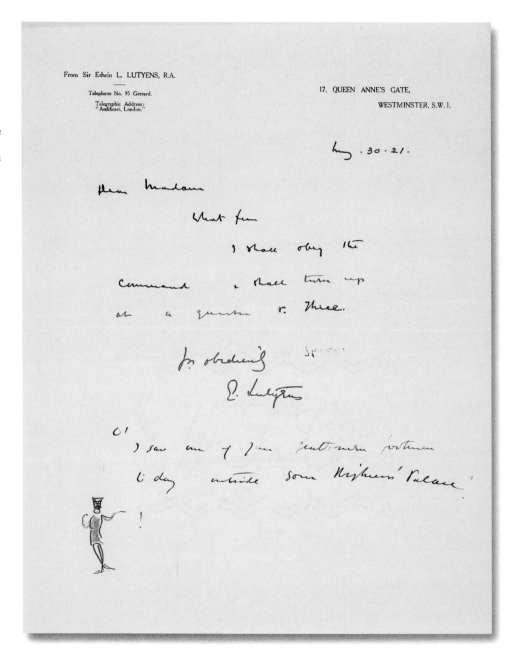

TEL: LEZANNICK.

Dec: 23
19^21

TRELASKE
N? LAUNCESTON
CORNWALL.

Dear Princess

It having been whispered that Her Majesty had mentioned She would like to have a little picture of herself in the style of the "orchestra" I had the pleasure of doing for the Dolls House, I determined to try & do something, &, if it turned out a failure — as is so often the case with any work — I'd say nothing about it. I now gather that that horrid fellow Lutyens has given away my very small secret, & fled to India, so that I cannot murder him — Yet! However, as I believe he has told Your Highness all about it, I am venturing to beg your

kind assistance, as in these wilds one can get nothing — What I want is a good photograph of Her Majesty ~~untouched~~ untouched if possible — in the position & light & shadow of the head indicated, if that is possible. I am trying to do a portrait of the Queen on the lines of a celebrated picture of one of her ancestors — so want the photograph as nearly as possible in the same pose & effect. If Your Highness does not happen to have such a photograph, please do not think of troubling about it, as it can stand over till we get back to London in the middle of Jan? —

Your Highness' most faithfully

A letter dated December 23rd 1921, from Sir Arthur Cope to Princess Marie Louise, outlining his plans (including a rough sketch) for a portrait of Queen Mary.

The Queen's Dolls' House
A List of the Honorary Officers
connected with the Dolls' House

| | |
|---|---|
| Architect | Sir Edwin Landseer Lutyens, Kt., R.A. |
| Draughtsman | F.B. Nightingale, A.R.I.B.A. |
| Engineer | A.J. Thomas, M.S.A. |
| Decorator and Upholsterer | George Muntzer |
| Librarian | H.H. Princess Marie Louise, G.B.E. |
| Musical Librarian | Mrs Adela Maddison |
| Cellarer | Francis L. Berry |
| Gardener | Miss Gertrude Jekyll |

The firm of Sangorski & Sutcliffe were responsible for the binding of the miniature library, a commission which gave them much pleasure, as this letter shows.

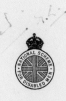

Telephone No:
2252 Gerrard.

Telegraphic Address:
"Bindristic.London"

F. Sangorski &
G. Sutcliffe.
Bookbinders.

George Sutcliffe.

1-5 Poland Street,
Oxford Street,
London, W.1.

March 11th 19 22

Her Highness The Princess Marie Louise.
        Ambassador's Court.
            St.James's Palace.
                S.W.


Madam,

        In the excitement of opening the box of
Original Manuscripts I overlooked your letter or
I would have at once assured you  that Mr. Lucas
was correct in expressing my desire to  offer my
services in the formation of Her Majesty's  miniature palace library.   It will be a pleasurable
holiday recreation from our hum-drum work and do
not hesitate to send me all you desire to  have
done though at the same time I would not wish to
deprive any of my colleagues of the joy of sharing
with me the binding of one of the most  wonderful
libraries in the world.  Mr. Kipling's manuscript
is really priceless.

        I beg to remain, Madam,

            Your Highness's Obedient Servant,

                George Sutcliffe.

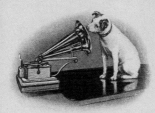

# The Gramophone Company ltd

BY APPOINTMENT TO H.M. QUEEN ALEXANDRA.

REF N° 812.

TELEPHONE: 180, SOUTHALL.
(TEN LINES.)

TELEGRAMS OR CABLES.
JABBERMENT HAYES, MIDDLESEX.

CODES
A B C 5TH EDITION, LIEBERS,
WESTERN UNION.

MANAGING DIRECTOR.
ALFRED CLARK.

IN YOUR REPLY
PLEASE REFER TO

AC/LN.

HIS MASTER'S VOICE.

HEAD OFFICE,

HAYES,

MIDDLESEX.

10th October 1922.

Sir Edwin L. Lutyens,   R.A.,
13 Mansfield Street,
LONDON,   W.1.

Dear Sir Edwin,

I have read of the Dolls House which you are preparing
and have heard of it from a number of artist friends, and I
have felt that there really should be a miniature gramophone
included to make it quite complete as an example of the present-
day home.   The difficulties of making a small model that would
work perfectly have seemed too great for me to suggest it to you
until now.

After a series of experiments in our laboratory we are
now quite sure that one can be made, and I feel safe in asking
you whether such a model would be acceptable from our Board of
Directors.   It would be to scale and of wood to match the other
miniature furniture of the room in which it would be placed,
and would have with it a series of tiny records.   These records
will reproduce quite well, and I had in mind having some of the
leading singers make them, as I feel sure they would be only too
delighted to do for such an object.

Knowing that you are probably overwhelmed with suggestions,
I have thought it better to write you in this way rather than to
ask for an appointment, but if you should care to see me I would,
of course, call on you.

Will you be good enough to let me know whether the gift
will be acceptable?

Yours faithfully,

Alfred Clark.

Managing Director.

This letter from The Gramophone Company, with its illustrated heading of Nipper listening to His Master's Voice, demonstrates that contributions to the House were not just requested, but sometimes volunteered.

The handwriting of Edmund Dulac was evidently almost as artistic as the decoration he provided for the walls of The Nursery and the Queen's Boudoir.

TEL. PARK 5328.

117, LADBROKE ROAD,
HOLLAND PARK, W.

Nov. 27ᵗʰ 1922.

Madam,

Waring & Gillows have started on the furniture for H.M. The Queen's Chinese boudoir, and I should like to know what colour of lacquer Her Majesty prefers. I wonder if anything interesting could be done in ivory white with silver & black?

I am at present in the midst of the fairy tales for the nursery, and wish the days were twice as long.

with Kindest wishes

yours respectfully,

Edmund Dulac

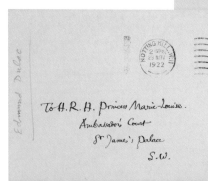

Edmund Dulac

To H.R.H. Princess Marie-Louise.
Ambassador's Court
St James's Palace
S.W.

Bibliography

Her Highness Princess Marie Louise, *My Memories of Six Reigns*,
London 1956

Hussey, C., *The Queen's Dolls House. The Palace of Their Majesties
The King and Queen of Lilliput*, London 1924

Murray, J. *Edwin Lutyens by his daughter* Mary Lutyens,
London 1980

Pope-Hennessy, J., *Queen Mary 1867–1953*, London 1959

*The Letters of Sir Edwin Lutyens to his wife Lady Emily*,
edited by Clayre Percy Jane Ridley, London 1985

Robinson, J.M., *Queen Mary's Dolls' House Official Guidebook*,
London 2004, repr. 2006, 2009

Stewart-Wilson, M. *Queen Mary's Dolls' House*, London 1988,
repr. 1989, 1995, 1998 and 2000

*The Heavenly Mansions (and other essays on architecture)*,
edited by John Summerson, London 1949, repr. 1998

Published by Royal Collection Enterprises Ltd
St James's Palace, London SW1A 1JR

For a complete catalogue of current publications, please write to the address above,
or visit our website at www.royalcollection.org.uk

First published by Royal Collection Publications 2010. Reprinted 2010.

ISBN 978 1 905686 26 1

British Library Cataloguing in Publication Data: A catalogue record for this book is available
from the British Library.

Designed by Mick Keates
Production management by Debbie Wayment
Colour reproduction by Altaimage, London
Printed on 157gsm GS Chinese matt art
Printed and bound by C&C Offset Printing Co. Ltd

PICTURE CREDITS

All photography David Cripps, excepting copper kettle, p.36; Adrian Stokes' Landscape, p.43;
despatch box, p.73; illustrations to J. Smith, p.103 and all of the miniature works of art depicted in
Chapter 5: The Library & Art Collection.

All works reproduced are in the Royal Collection unless indicated otherwise below. Royal Collection
Enterprises are grateful for permission to reproduce the following:

P.11 A.C. Benson, Lawrence Weaver, E.V. Lucas and p.14 Sir George Frampton © National Portrait
Gallery, London; p.16 Gertrude Jekyll © GWI/Country Life/IPC; p.26 The Dolls' House in Lutyens'
home, Mansfield Street; p.80 E.F. Benson and p.98 George Bernard Shaw, Hilaire Belloc and
G.K. Chesterton © Hulton Archive/Getty Images; p.100 Sir John Bland-Sutton © Wellcome Library,
London; p.105 *Dymchurch Wall* © Tate, London, 2010; p.124 © Adam Pallant.

Every effort has been made to contact copyright holders; any omissions are inadvertent, and will be
corrected in future editions if notification of the amended credit is sent to the publisher in writing.

ACKNOWLEDGEMENTS

The permission of Her Majesty The Queen to reproduce items from the Royal Collection and the
Royal Archives is gratefully acknowledged.

My heartfelt thanks go firstly to Sir Hugh and Lady Roberts, with three cheers for Claire Allan,
Matt Ridley, John Martin Robinson and Perry Worsthorne for their kind encouragement and help.
I would also like to thank the following people from the Royal Collection: Nina Chang and Jacky
Colliss Harvey for their management of this project, Beth Clackett, Kate Heard, Sabrina Mackenzie,
Jonathan Marsden and the photographic services team.

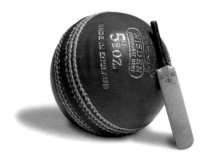

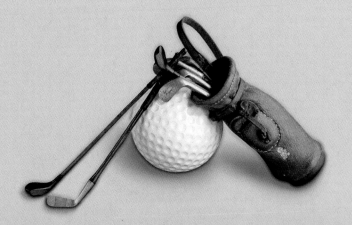